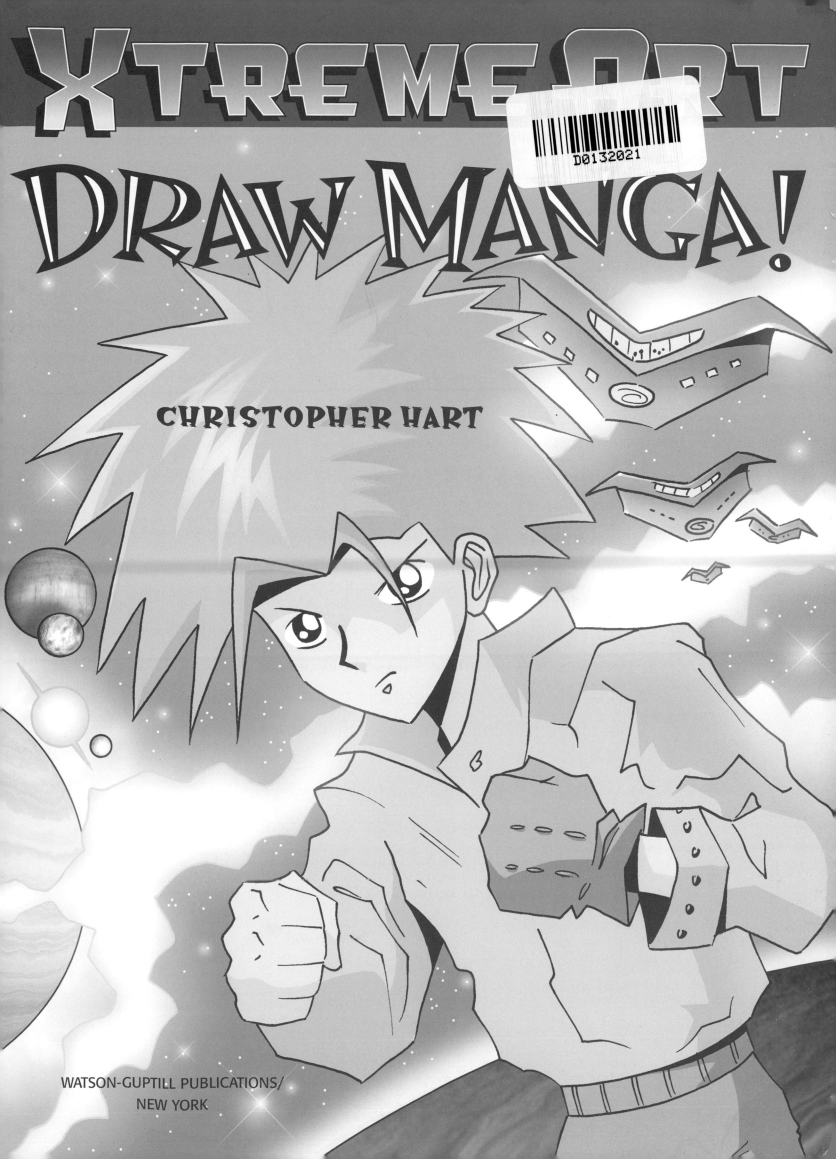

XTREME ART

DRAW MANGA!

CHRISTOPHER HART

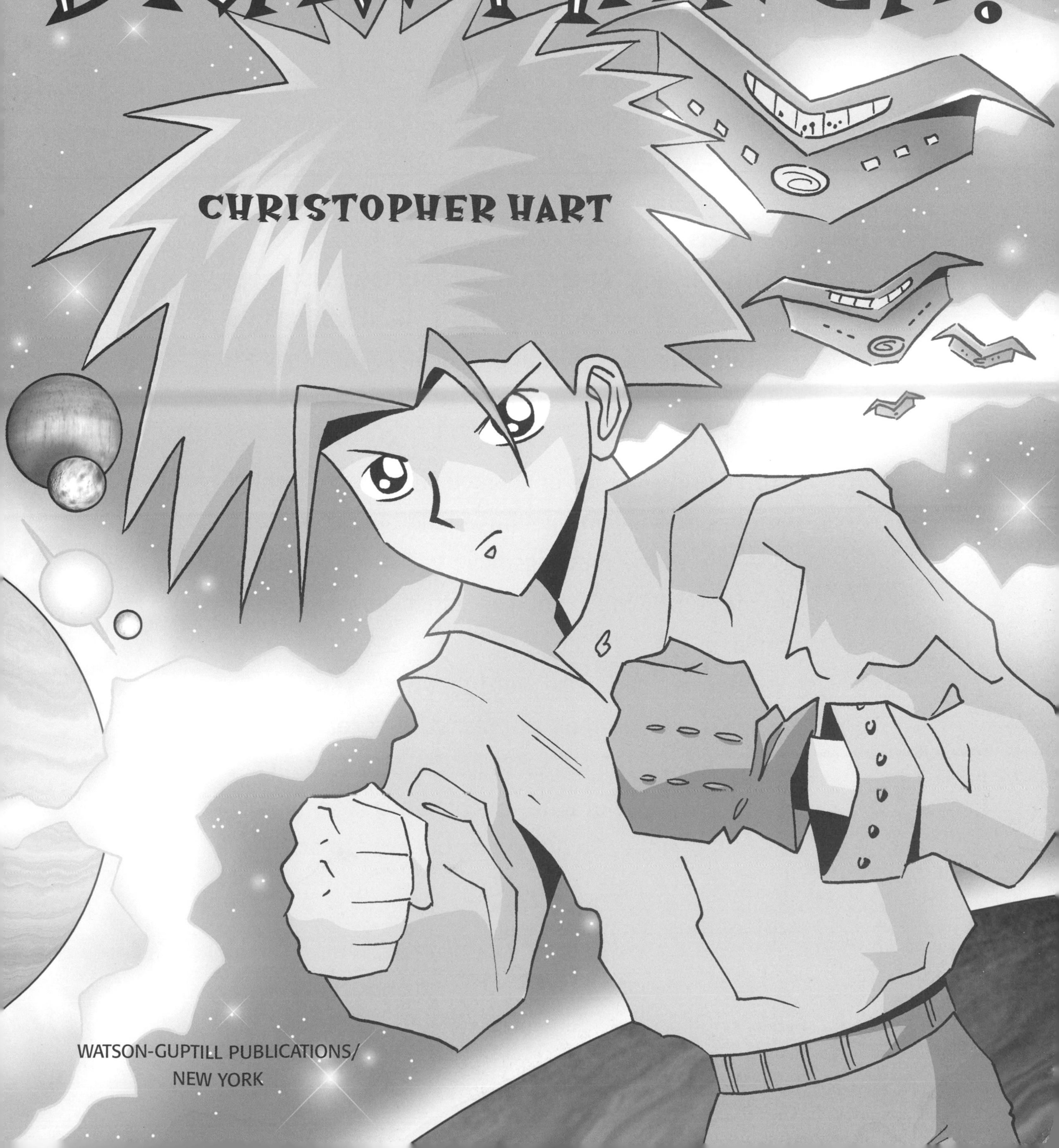

WATSON-GUPTILL PUBLICATIONS/
NEW YORK

INTRODUCTION

I've written many books that teach young artists, like yourself, how to draw. But I am especially proud of this series, *Xtreme Art.* These books use a special technique that will help you draw all kinds of cool characters quickly and easily!

Each drawing is broken down into four easy steps. Start by tracing or drawing step 1. Then just add the new lines in steps 2, 3, and 4. Before you know it you'll have drawn characters that would normally take much longer!

You'll find all kinds of characters to draw, starting with easier ones and getting a little harder as you go. A few of the drawings have backgrounds added (just for fun!), which you can either draw or trace if you like.

Manga is a Japanese word that means "comics." Manga is an extremely popular style of cartooning, known for the huge eyes of its characters. Manga began in Japan but it has become a craze that has swept the globe. So if drawing big-eyed, manga-style characters sounds like fun to you, just turn the page and let the adventure begin!

Tips for Using This Book

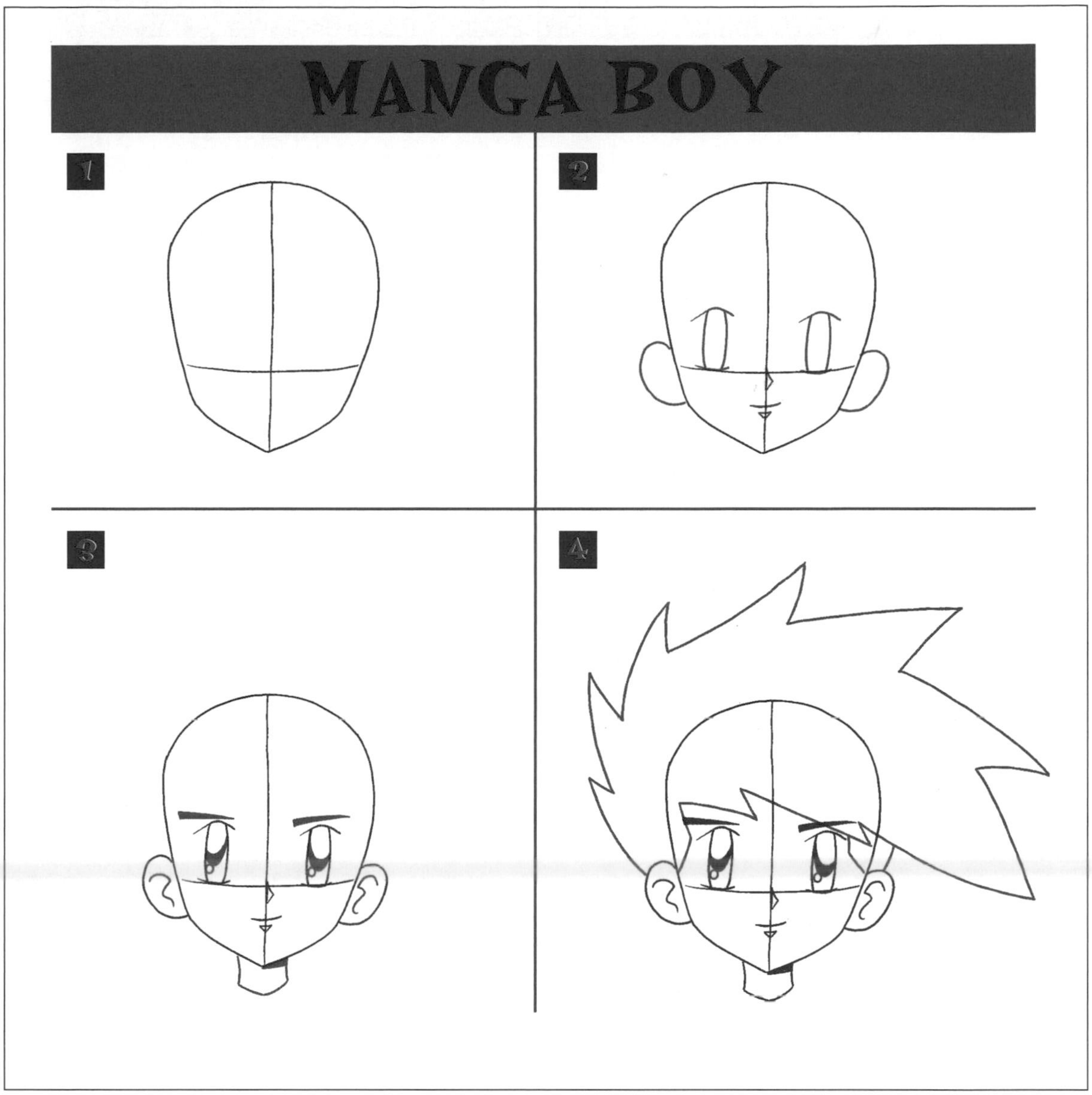
MANGA BOY
1
2
3
4

Trace or draw what you see in step 1. Then add the new lines (shown in red) in steps 2, 3, and 4. Draw with a light, sketchy line. Don't worry about getting it perfect on the first try.

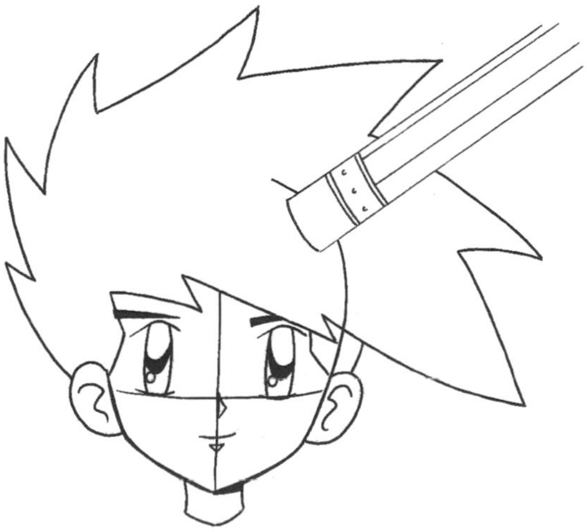

When you've finished the steps, erase the guidelines (the criss-crosses) and any other lines you don't want to keep. Go over the other lines to make them darker.

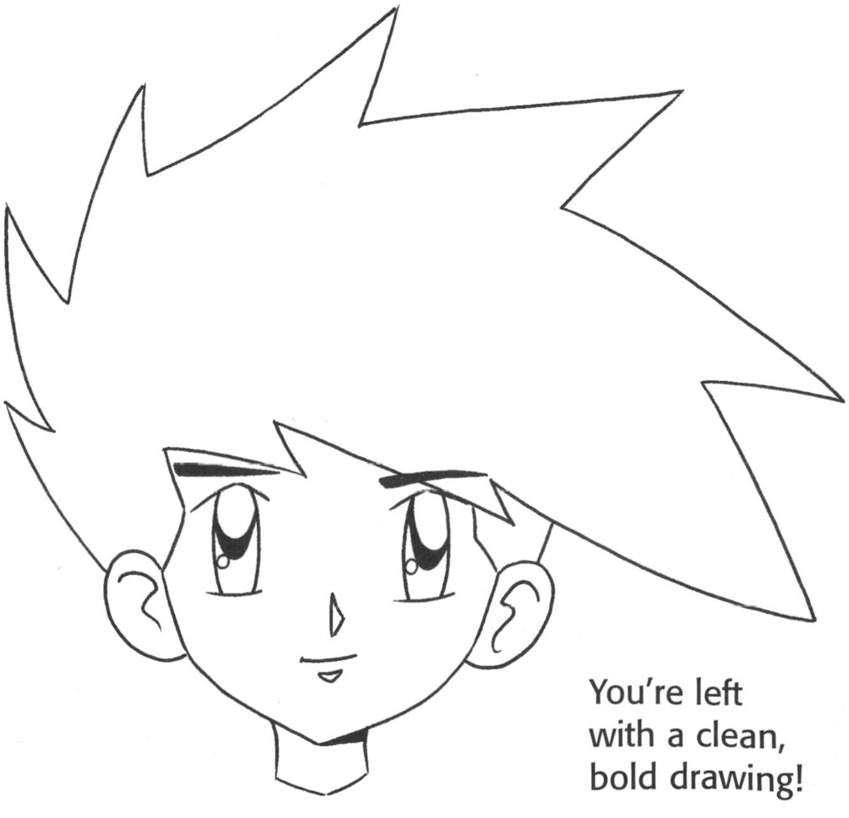

You're left with a clean, bold drawing!

THE BASICS

Let's start by going over some basics.

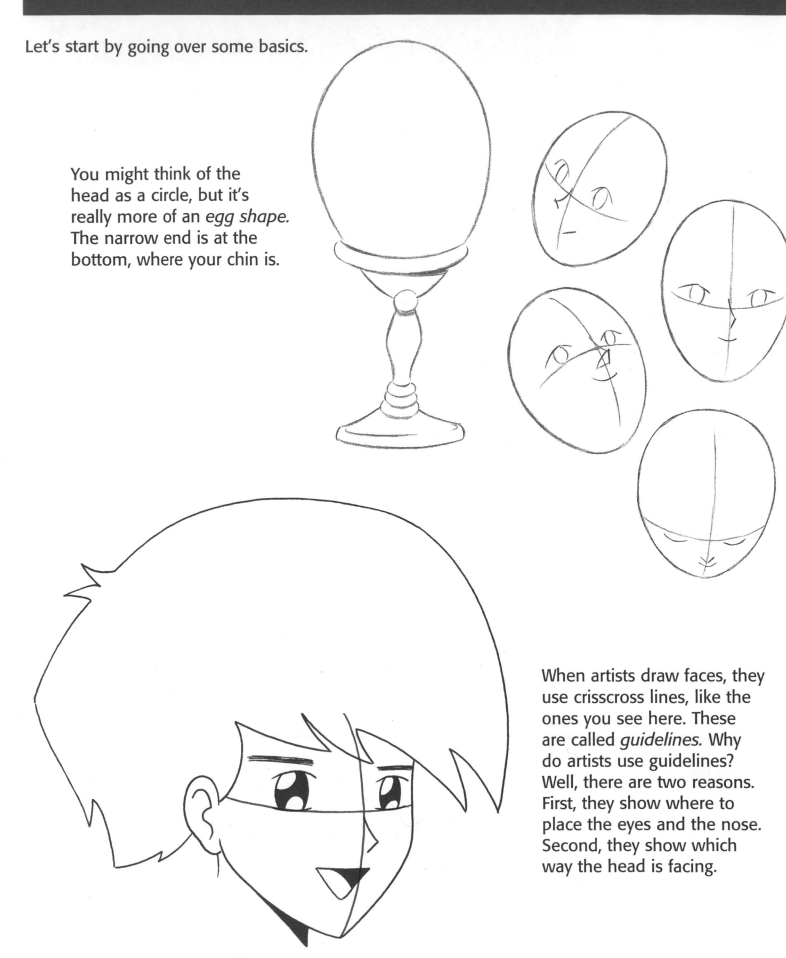

You might think of the head as a circle, but it's really more of an *egg shape.* The narrow end is at the bottom, where your chin is.

When artists draw faces, they use crisscross lines, like the ones you see here. These are called *guidelines.* Why do artists use guidelines? Well, there are two reasons. First, they show where to place the eyes and the nose. Second, they show which way the head is facing.

Manga characters are famous for their huge, shiny eyes. Now you're going to learn the secret to drawing them. It takes practice, but it's not hard to do. The first thing to remember is that the *shape* of the eyes changes with the *age* of the character.

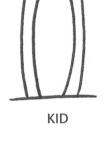

The Basic Shape of Each Eye

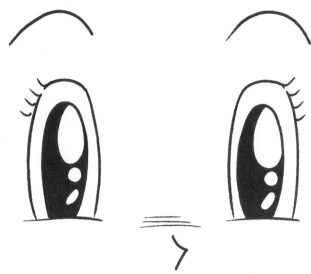

KID

Young characters have very tall eyes.

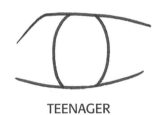

TEENAGER

Teenagers' eyes are big, but not as tall as kids' eyes.

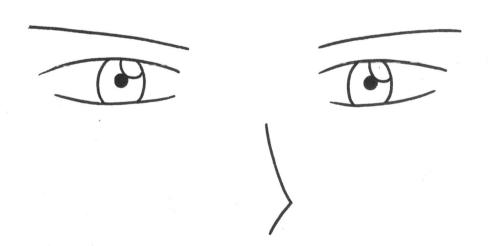

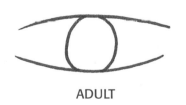

ADULT

Adults' eyes are the narrowest.

Here are some popular kinds of manga-style eyes. You can trace or draw these, or make up some of your own!

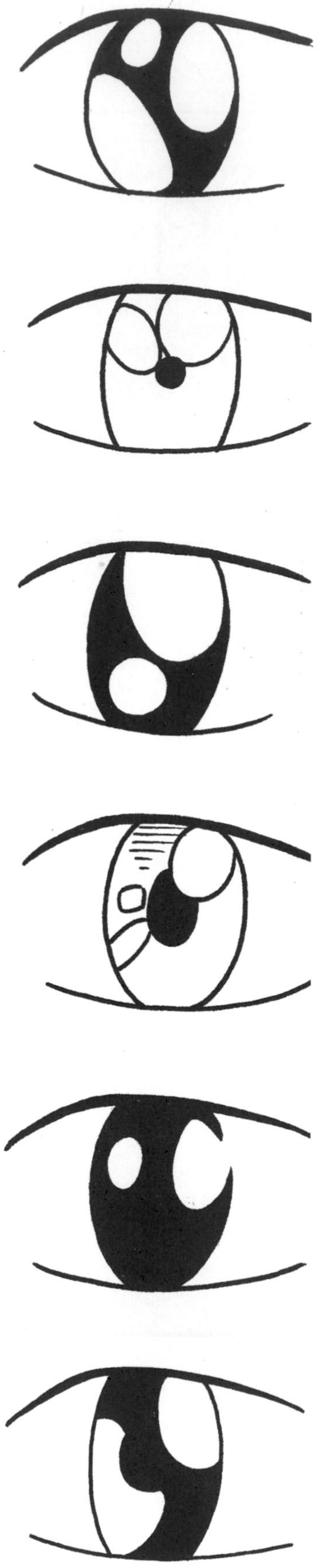

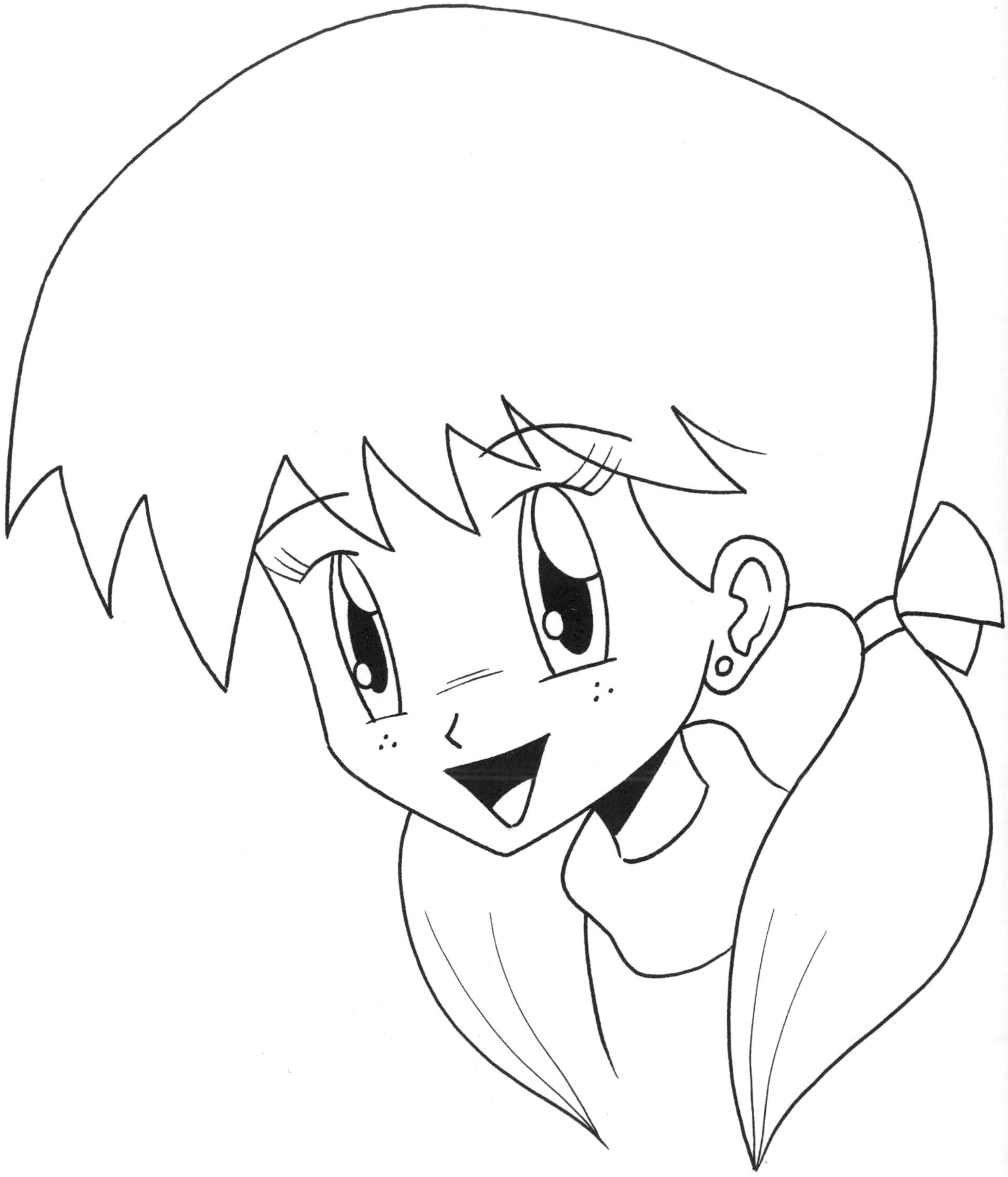

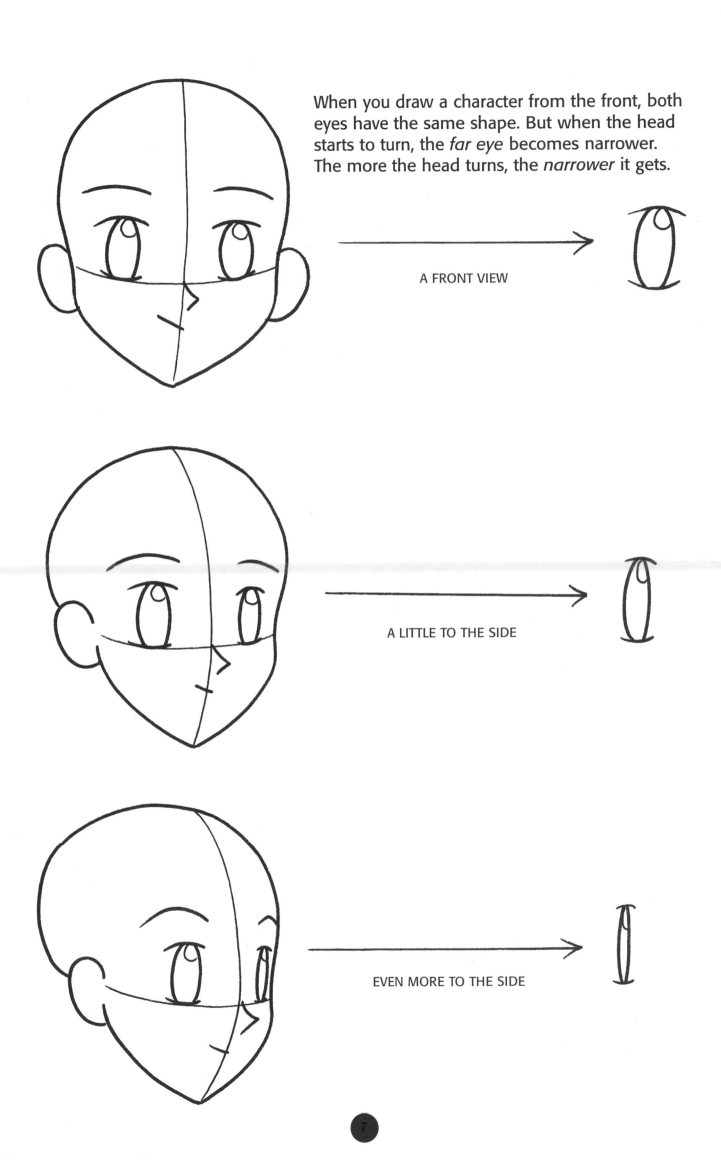

When you draw a character from the front, both eyes have the same shape. But when the head starts to turn, the *far eye* becomes narrower. The more the head turns, the *narrower* it gets.

A FRONT VIEW

A LITTLE TO THE SIDE

EVEN MORE TO THE SIDE

Hands can be hard to draw, so here are some tips to help you. Let's start with the back of the hand.

1. DRAW THE BACK OF THE HAND.

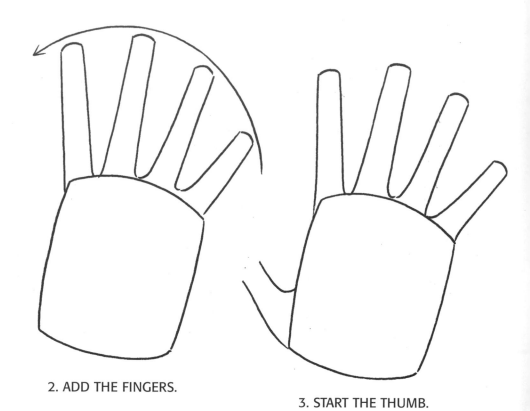

2. ADD THE FINGERS.

3. START THE THUMB.

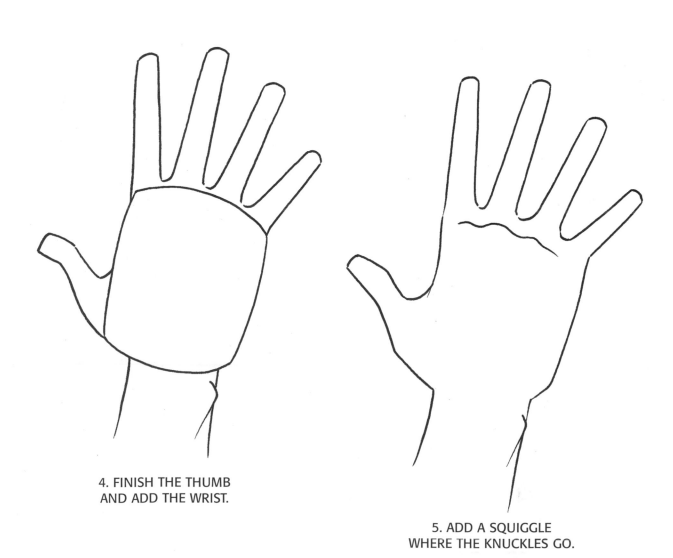

4. FINISH THE THUMB AND ADD THE WRIST.

5. ADD A SQUIGGLE WHERE THE KNUCKLES GO.

Now let's do the front of the hand.

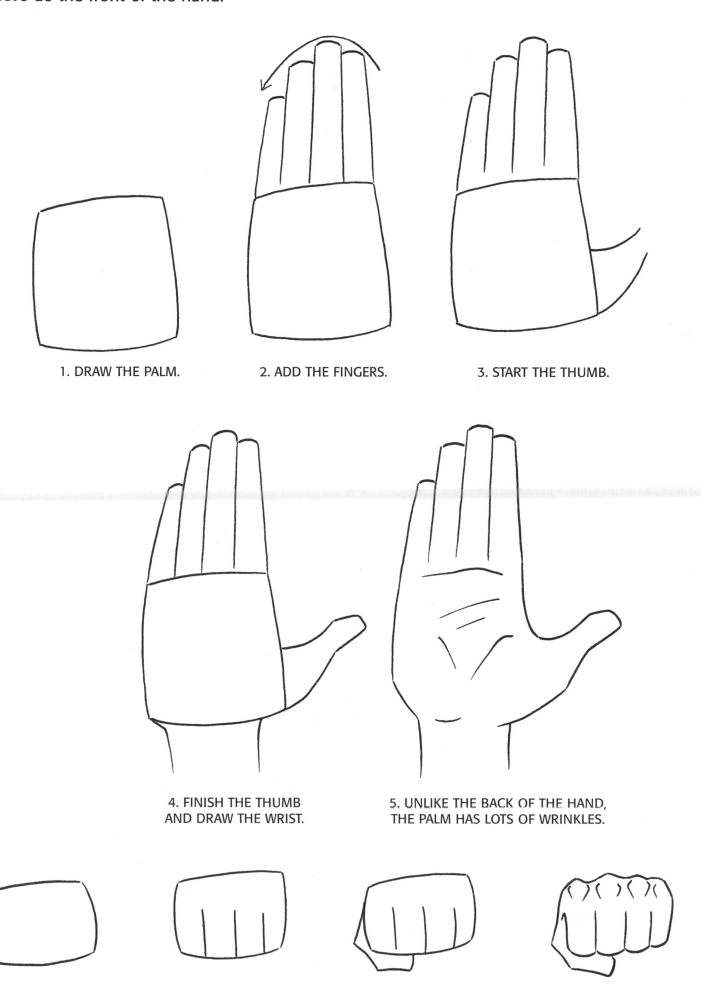

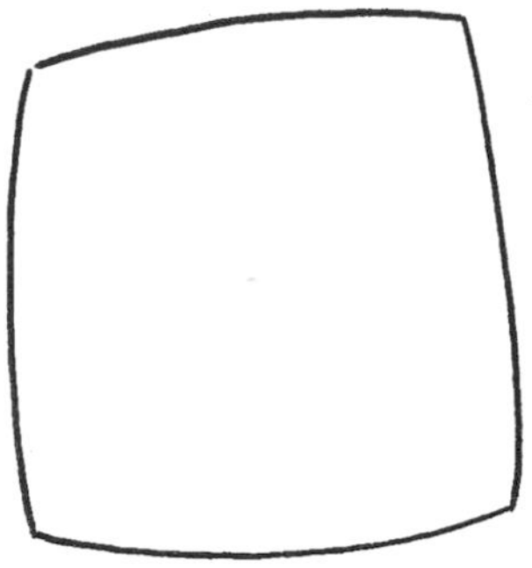

1. DRAW THE PALM.

2. ADD THE FINGERS.

3. START THE THUMB.

4. FINISH THE THUMB
AND DRAW THE WRIST.

5. UNLIKE THE BACK OF THE HAND,
THE PALM HAS LOTS OF WRINKLES.

Here are four steps for drawing a fist. The key to drawing a fist is getting the thumb right.

Hairstyles are very important in manga. They give each character a unique look. See how the same face looks different, just by changing the hairstyle? Remember, you don't have to copy my drawings exactly. It's perfectly okay to change my characters by making up your own manga hairstyles.

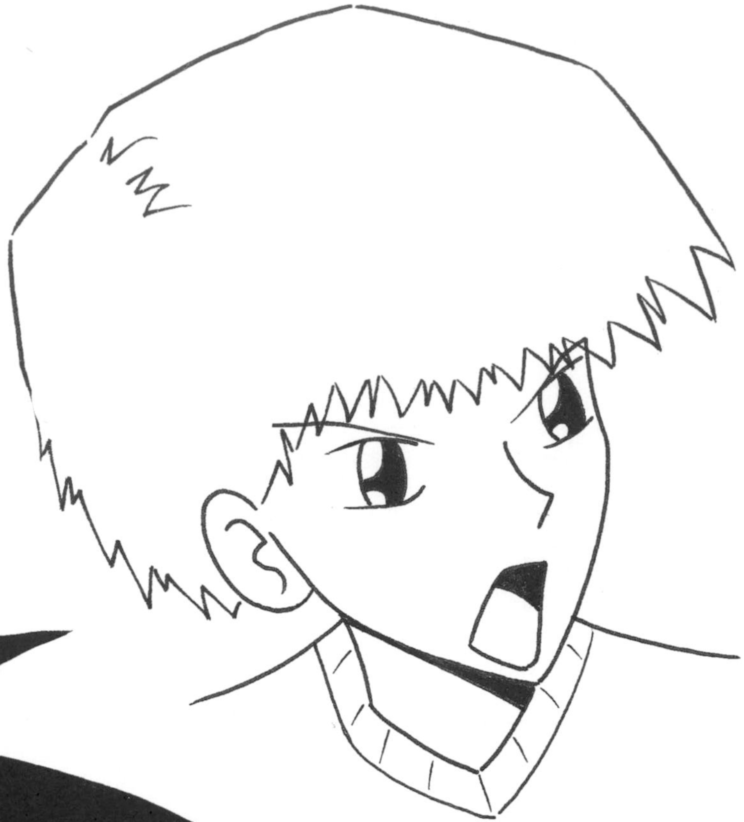

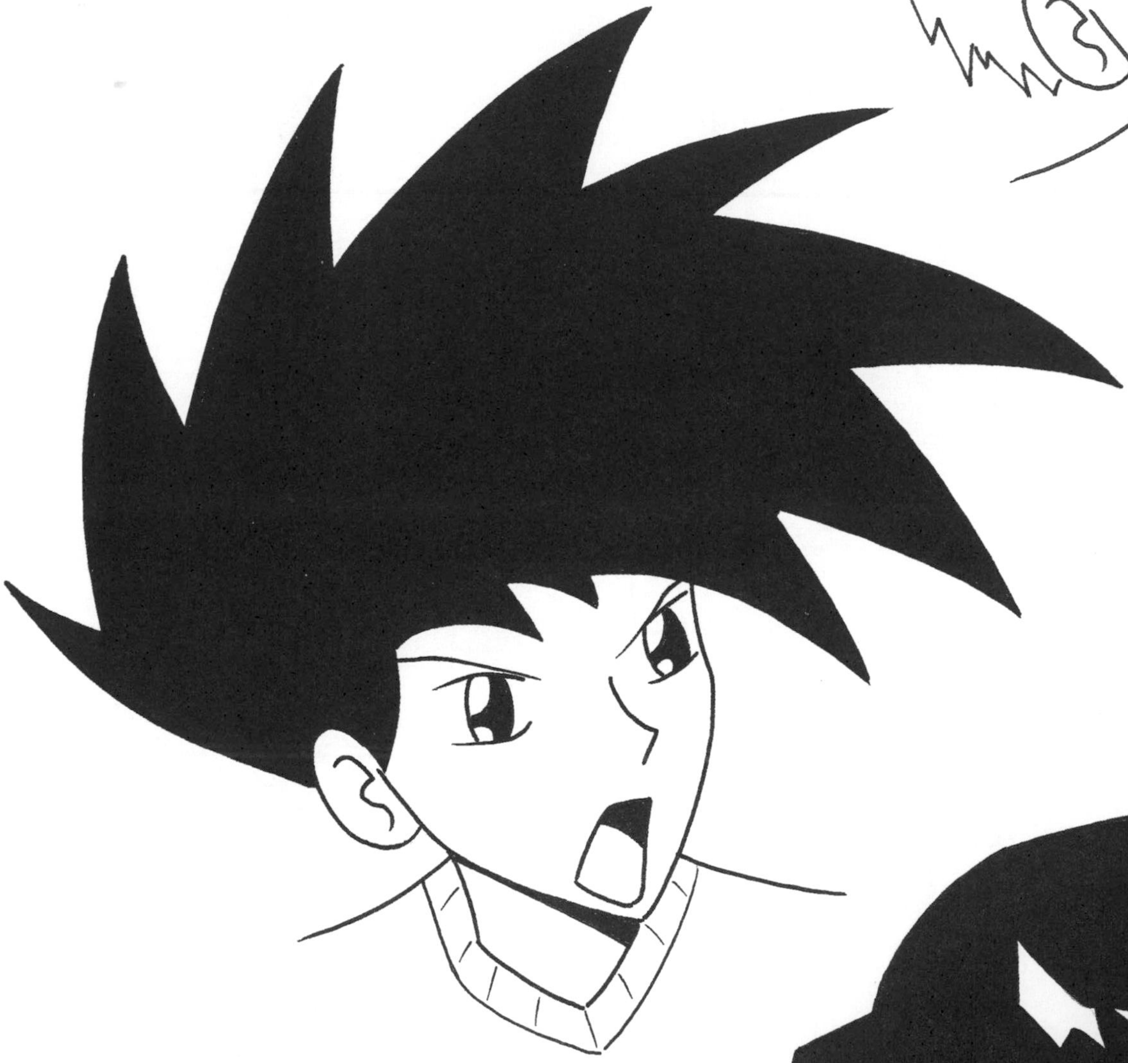

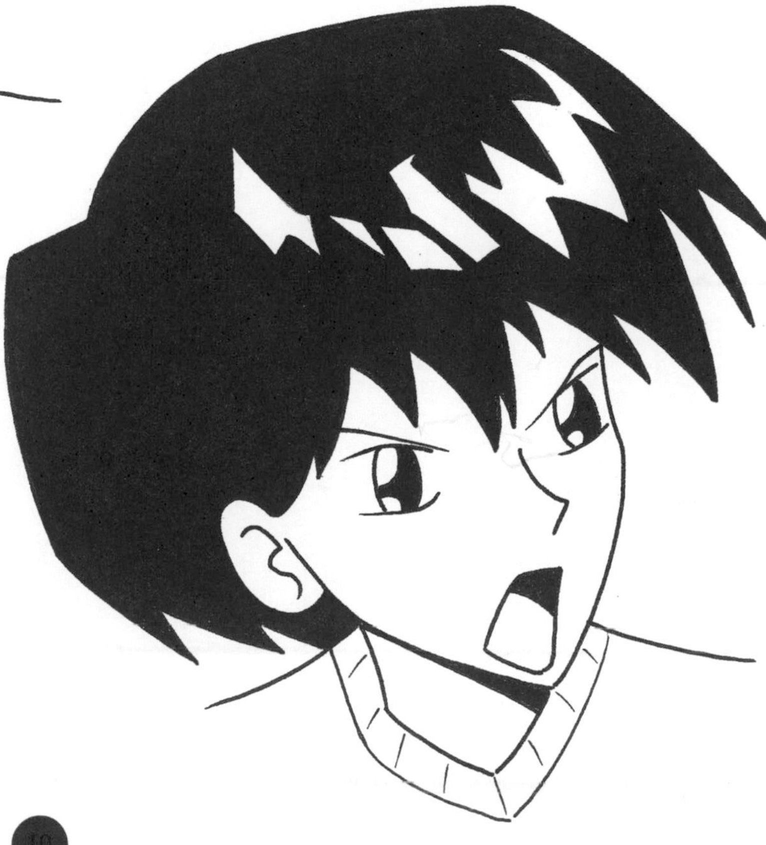

Here are a few more tips to help you. Take a look, then turn the page and start drawing!

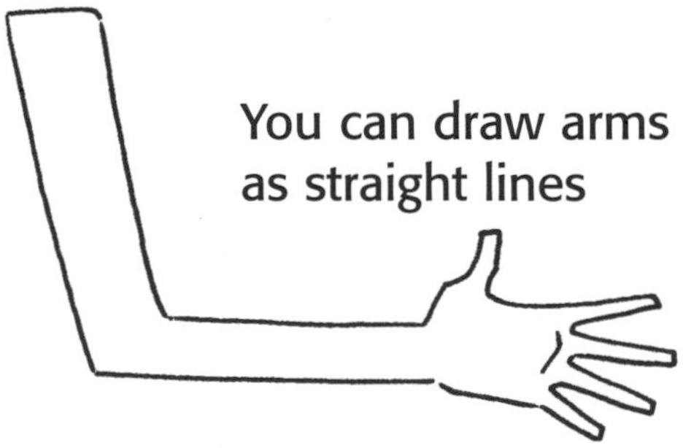

You can draw arms as straight lines

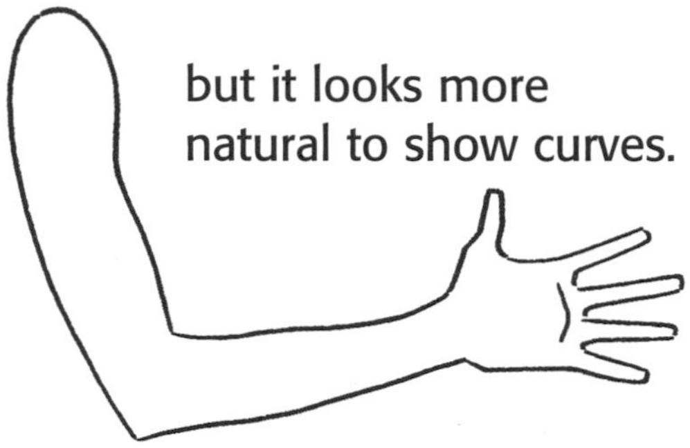

but it looks more natural to show curves.

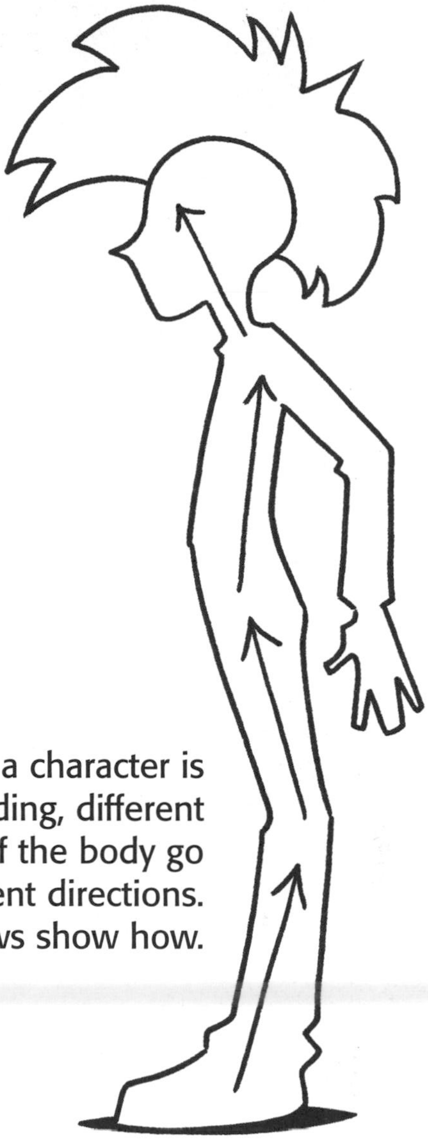

When a character is standing, different parts of the body go in different directions. These arrows show how.

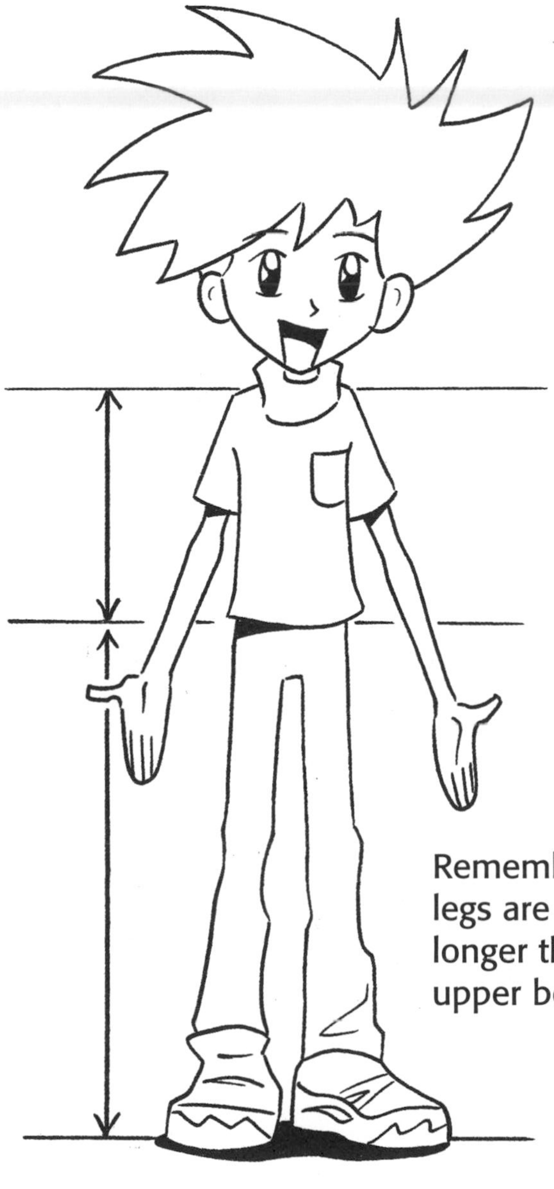

Remember that legs are *always* longer than the upper body.

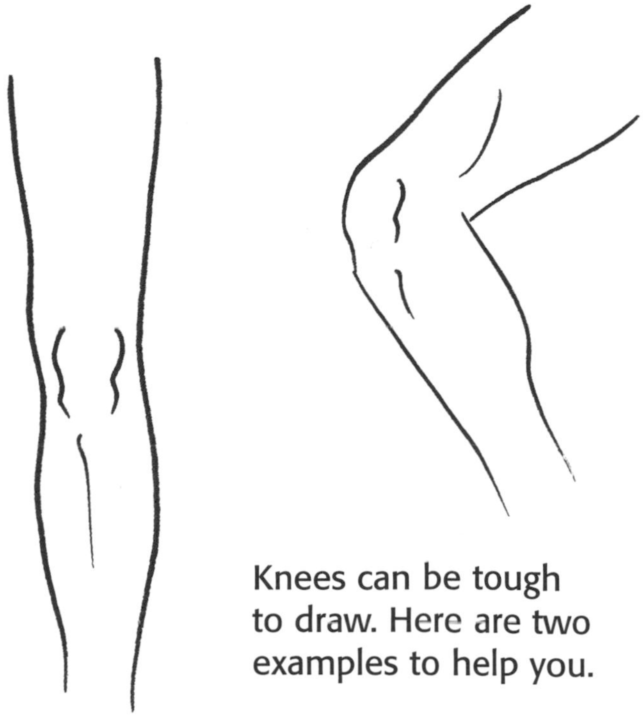

Knees can be tough to draw. Here are two examples to help you.

POPULAR BOY

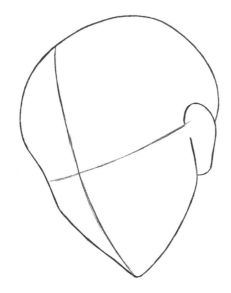

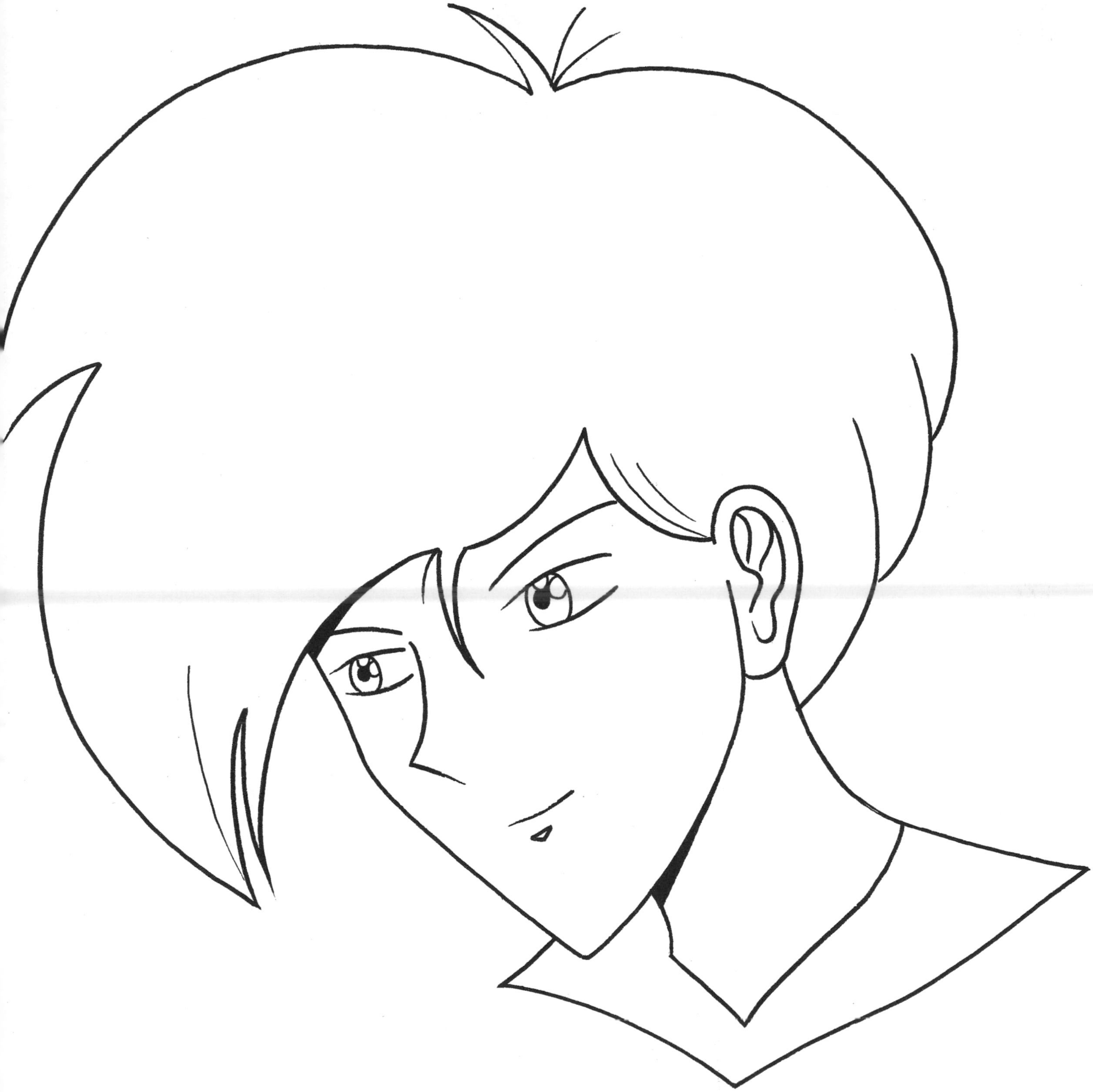

SCHOOLGIRL

1

2

3

4

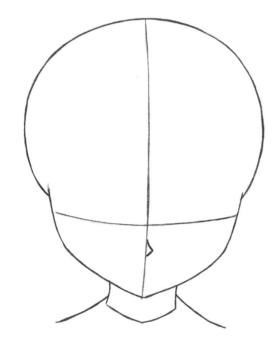

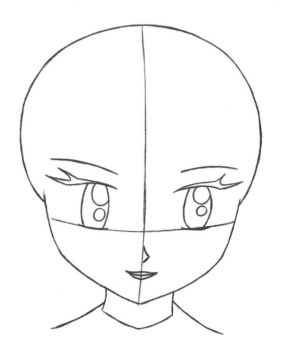

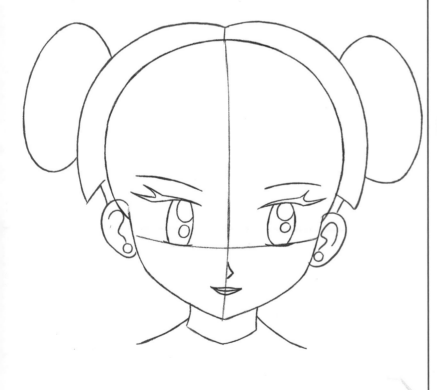

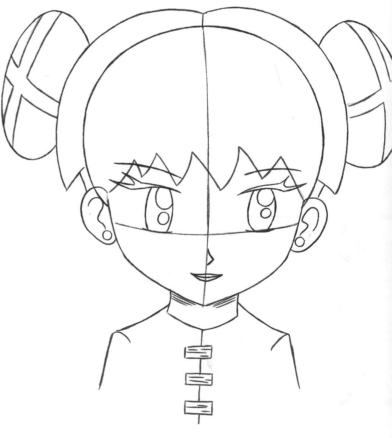

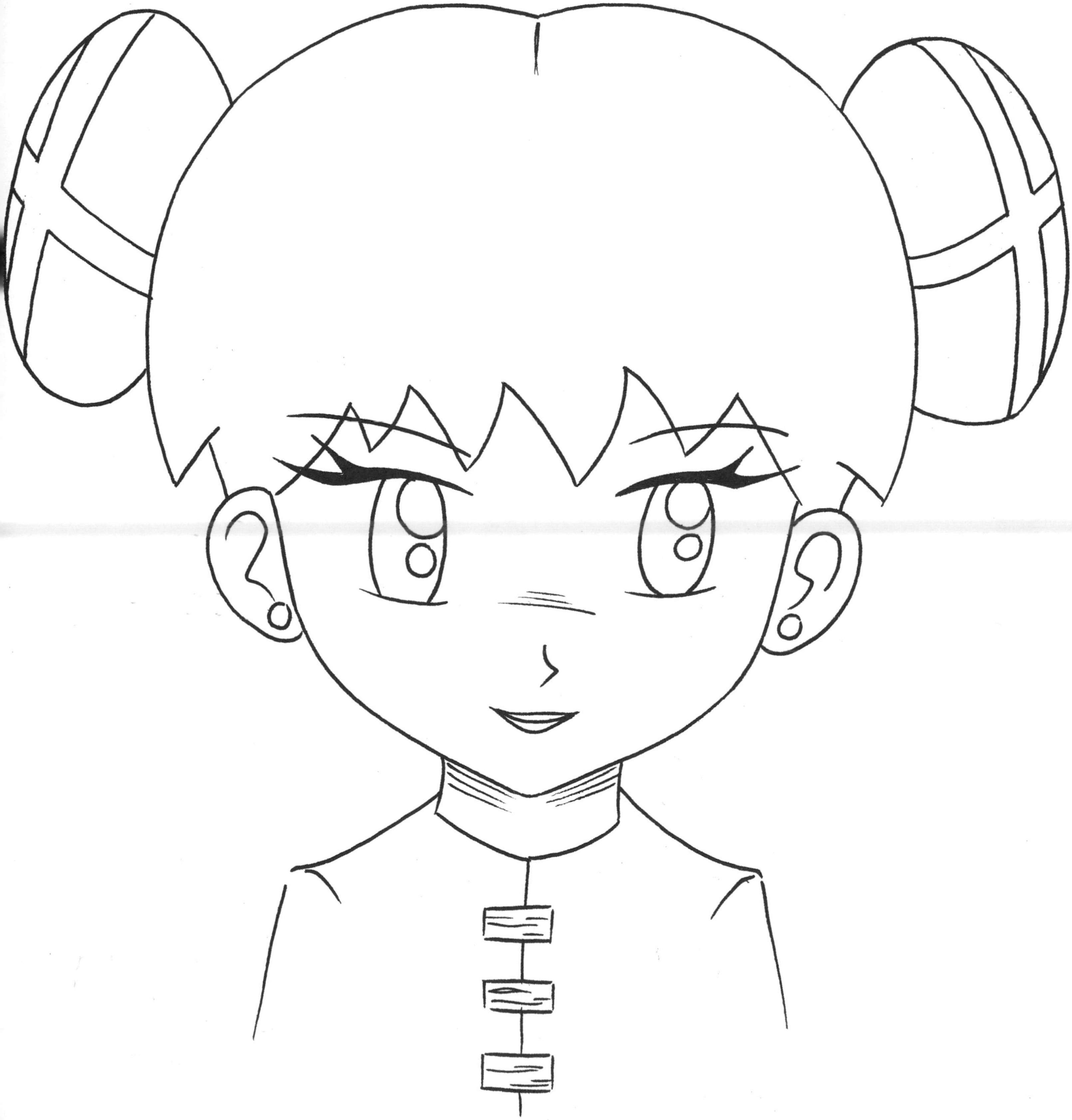

STARSHIP COMMANDER

1

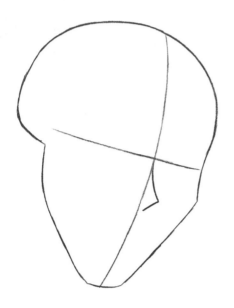

2

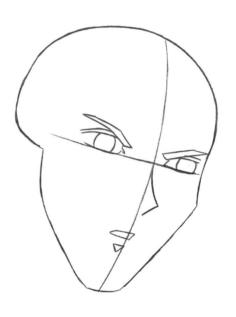

3

4

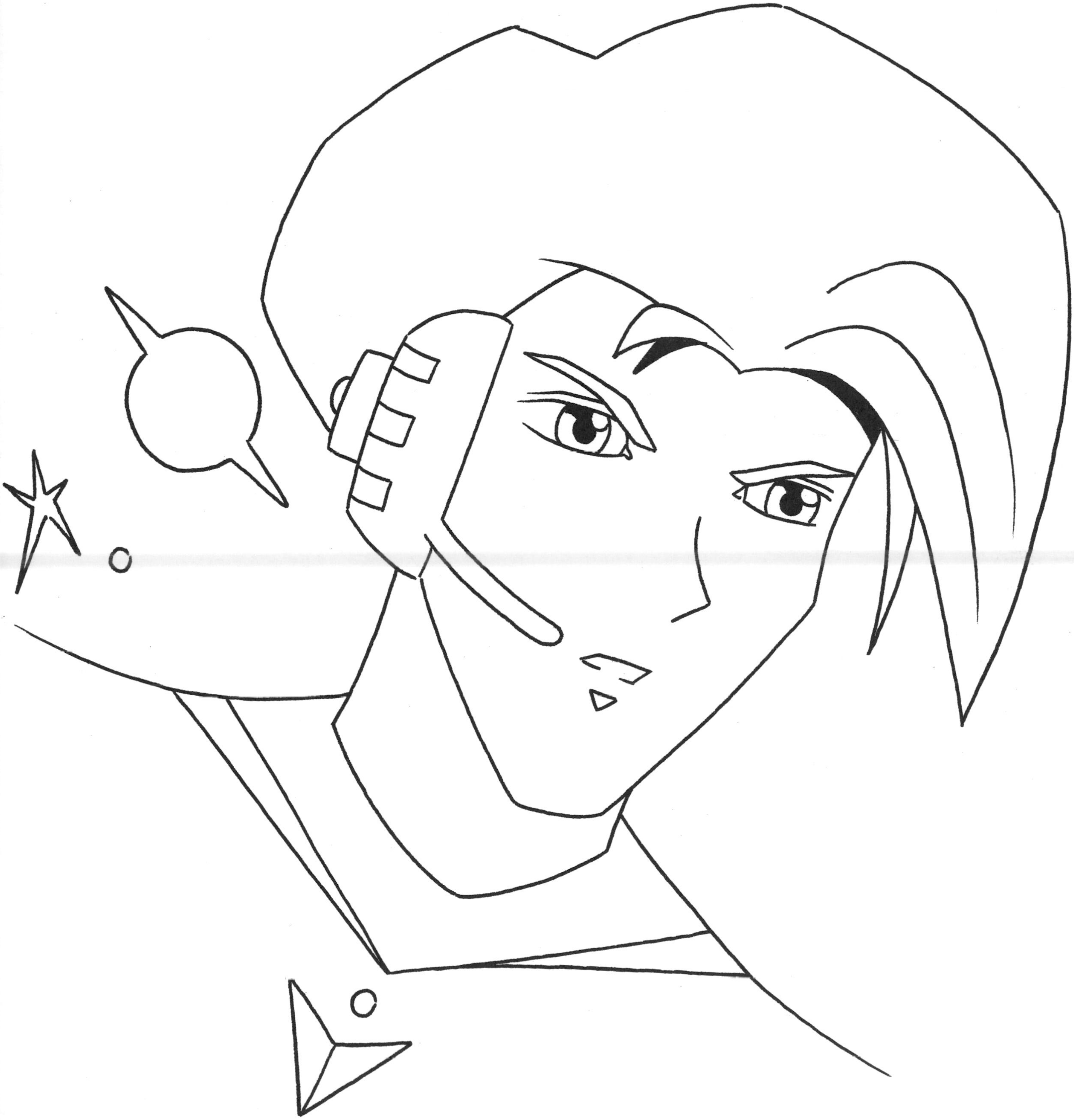

FASHION TEEN

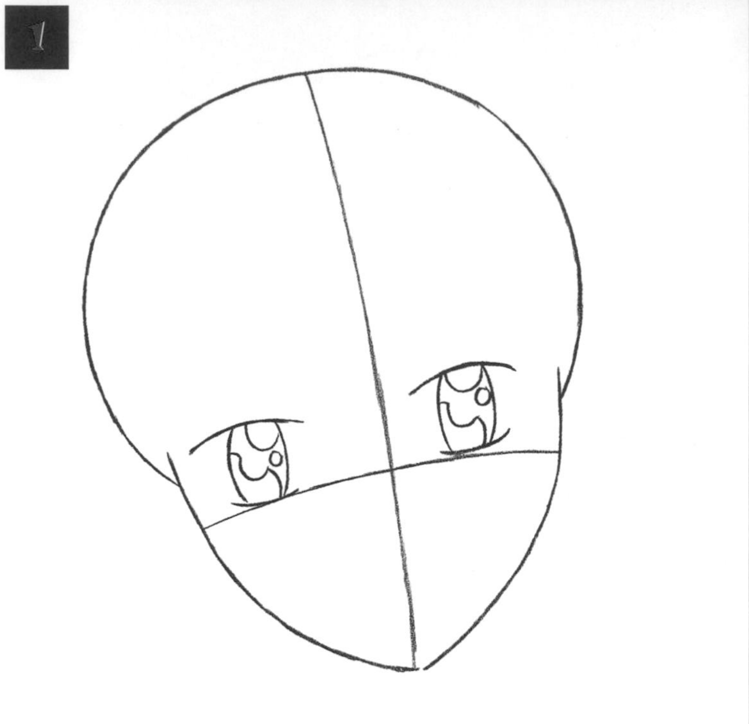
1

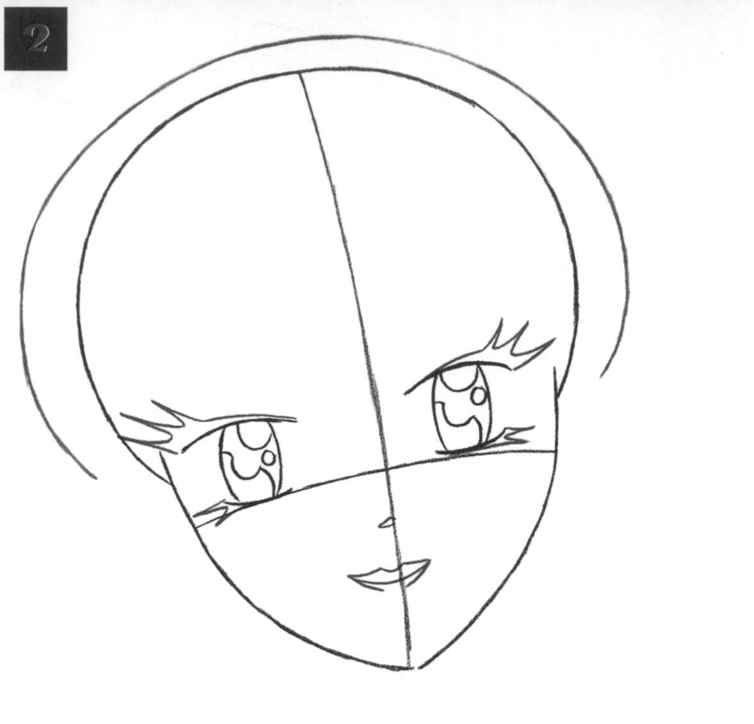
2

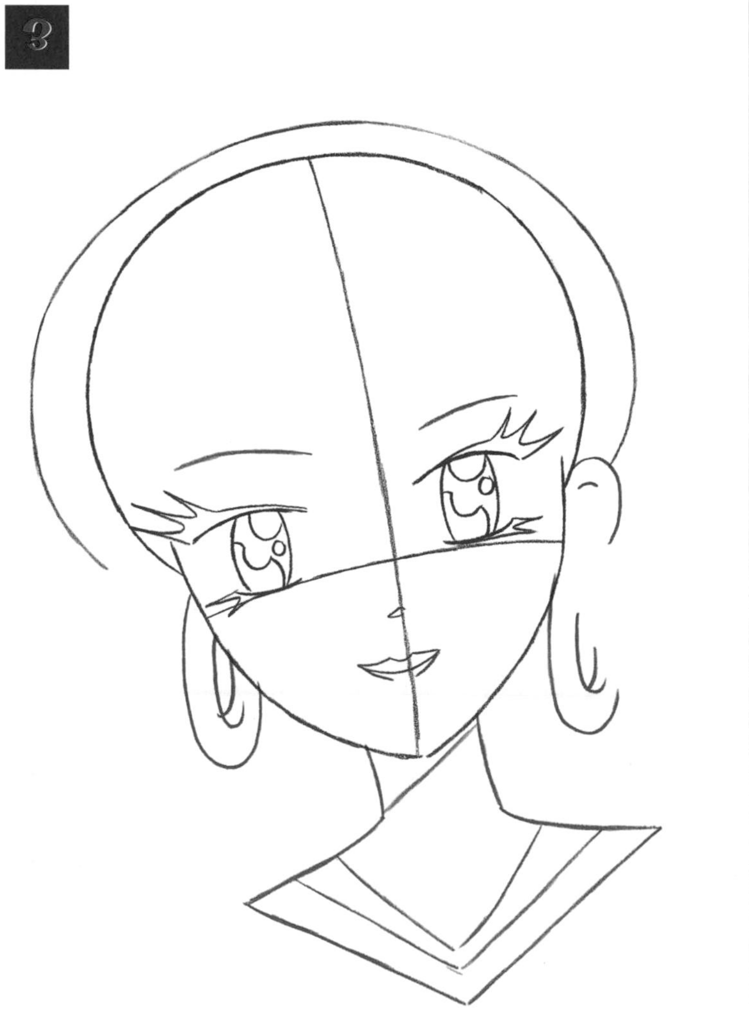
3

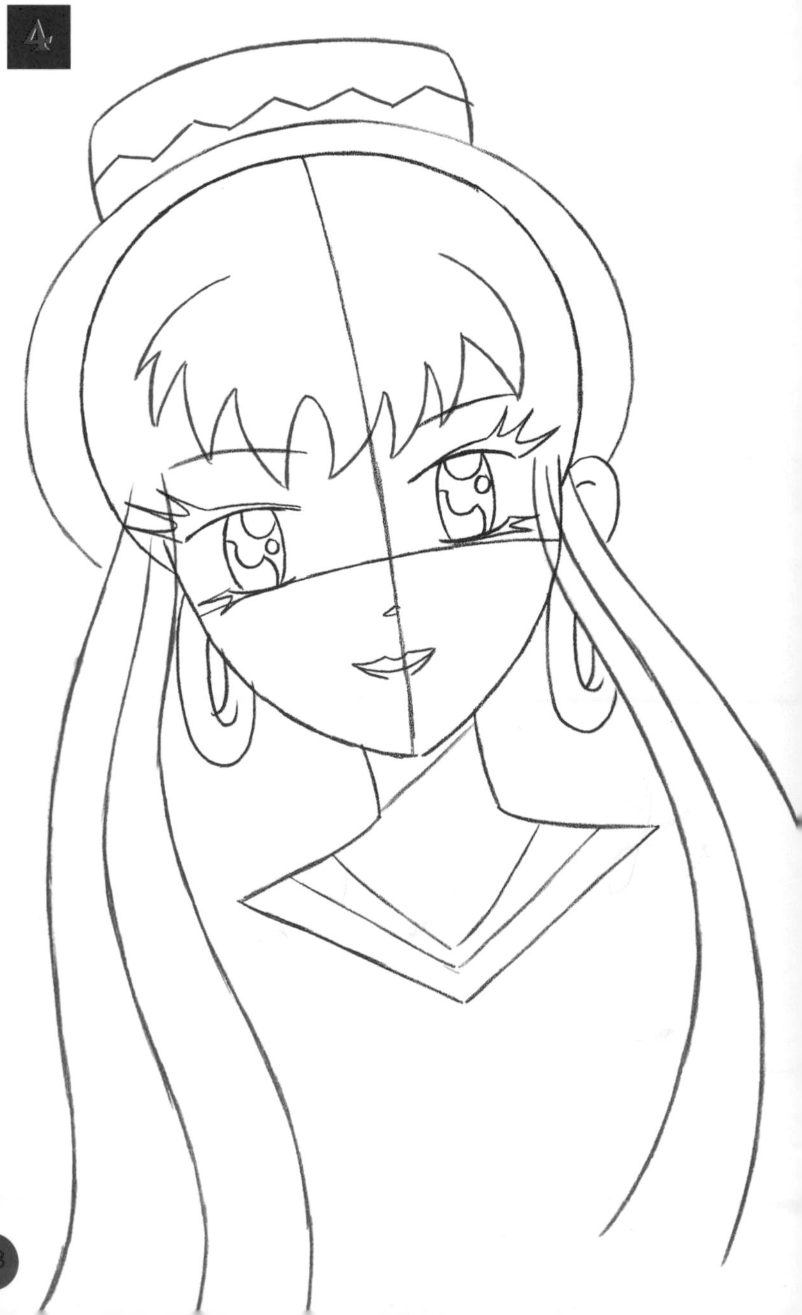
4

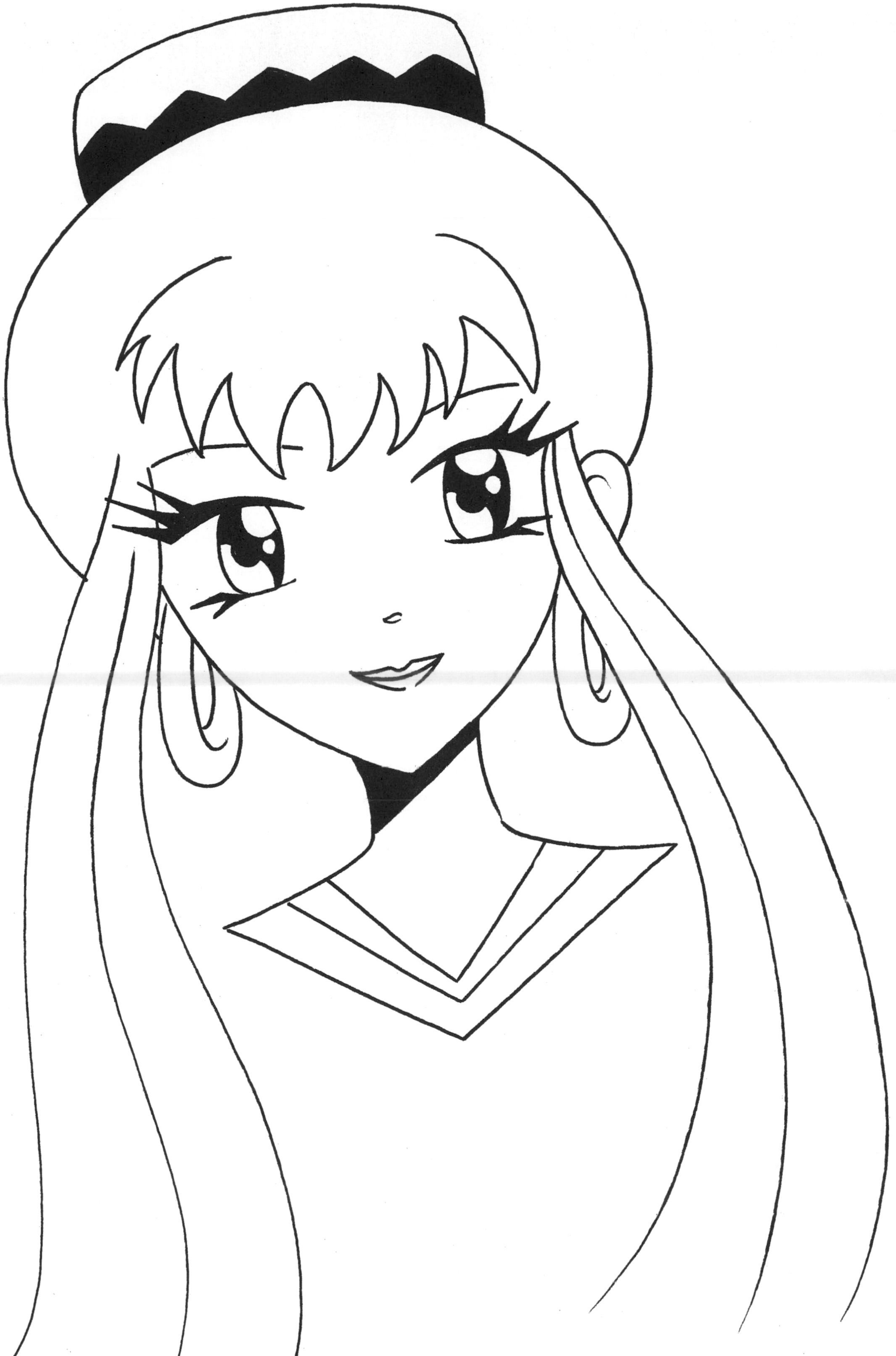

HIGH SCHOOL WARRIOR

1

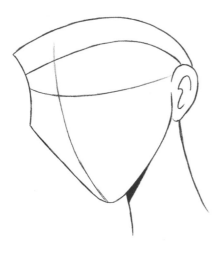

2

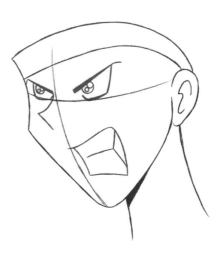

3

4

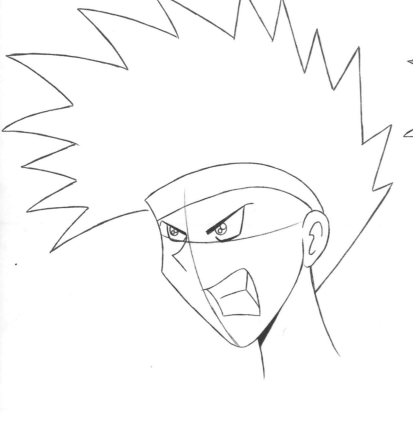

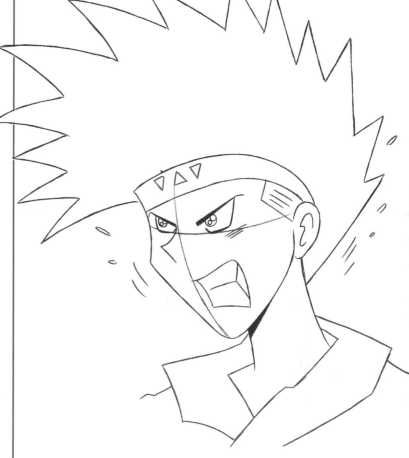

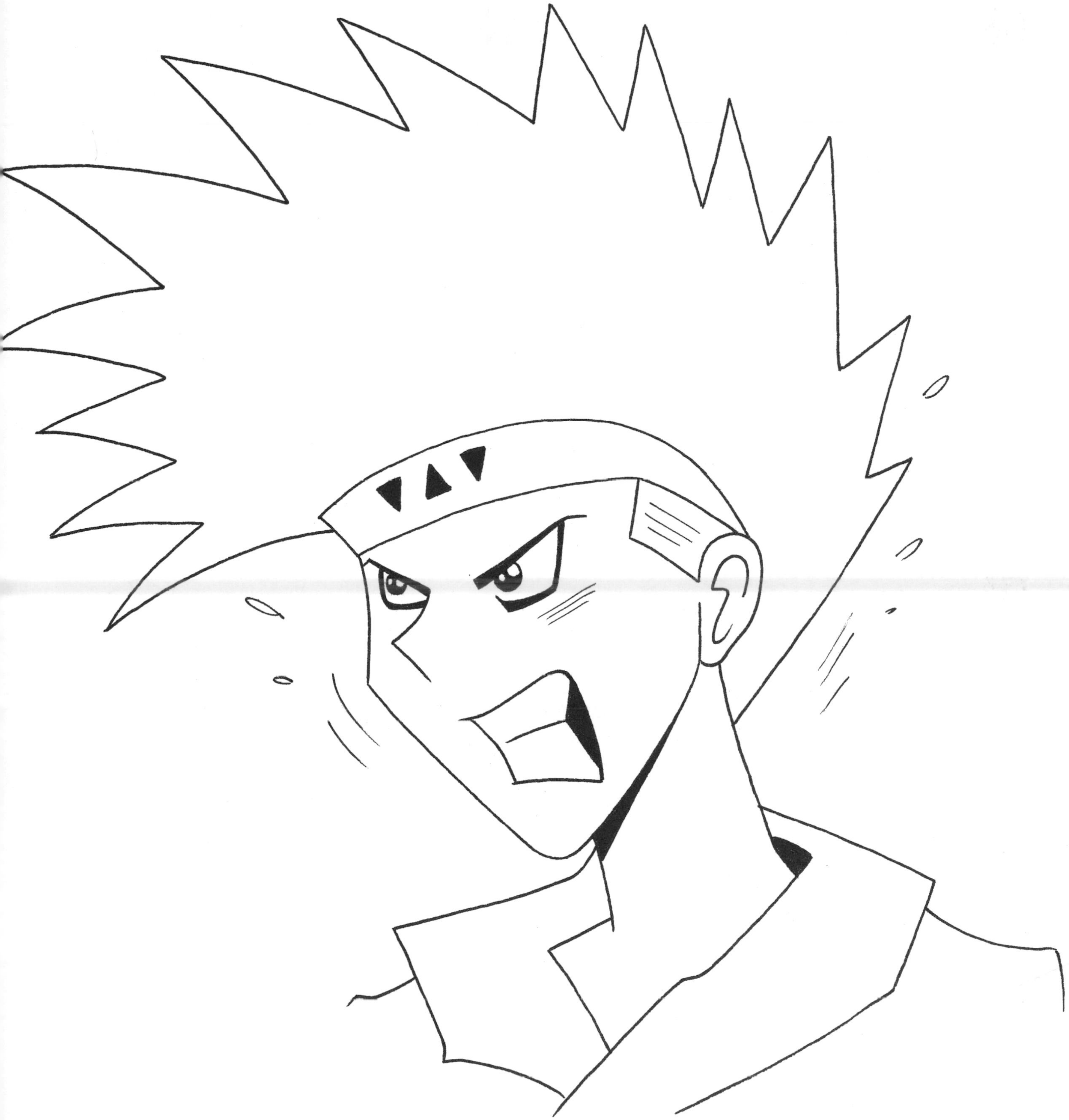

BIG GENERAL

1

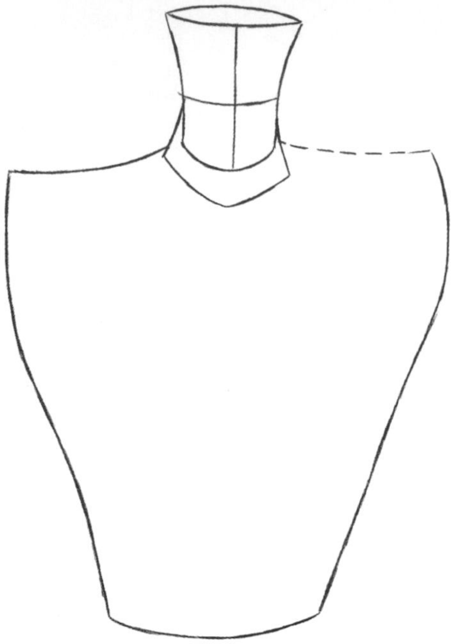

2

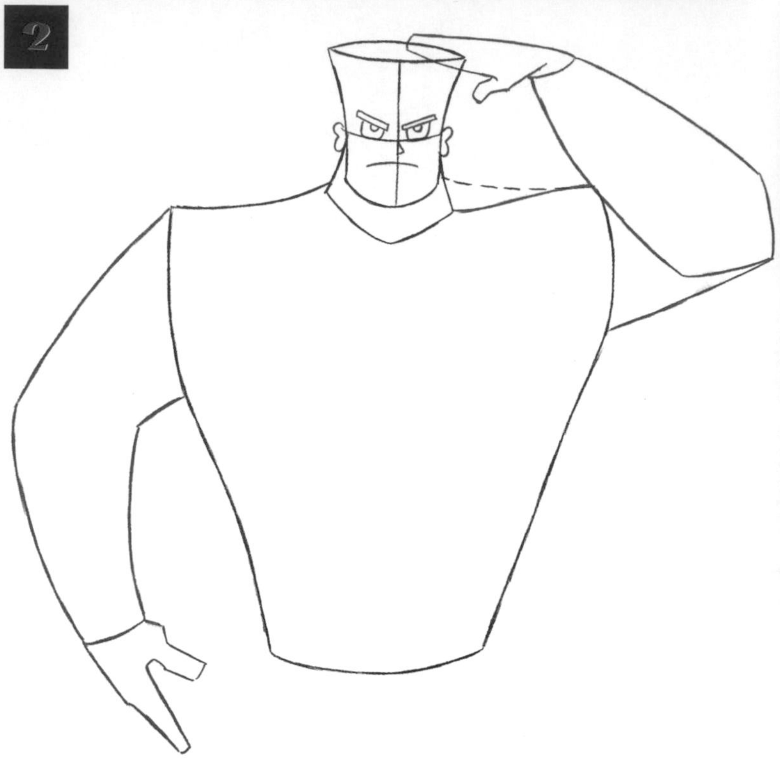

3

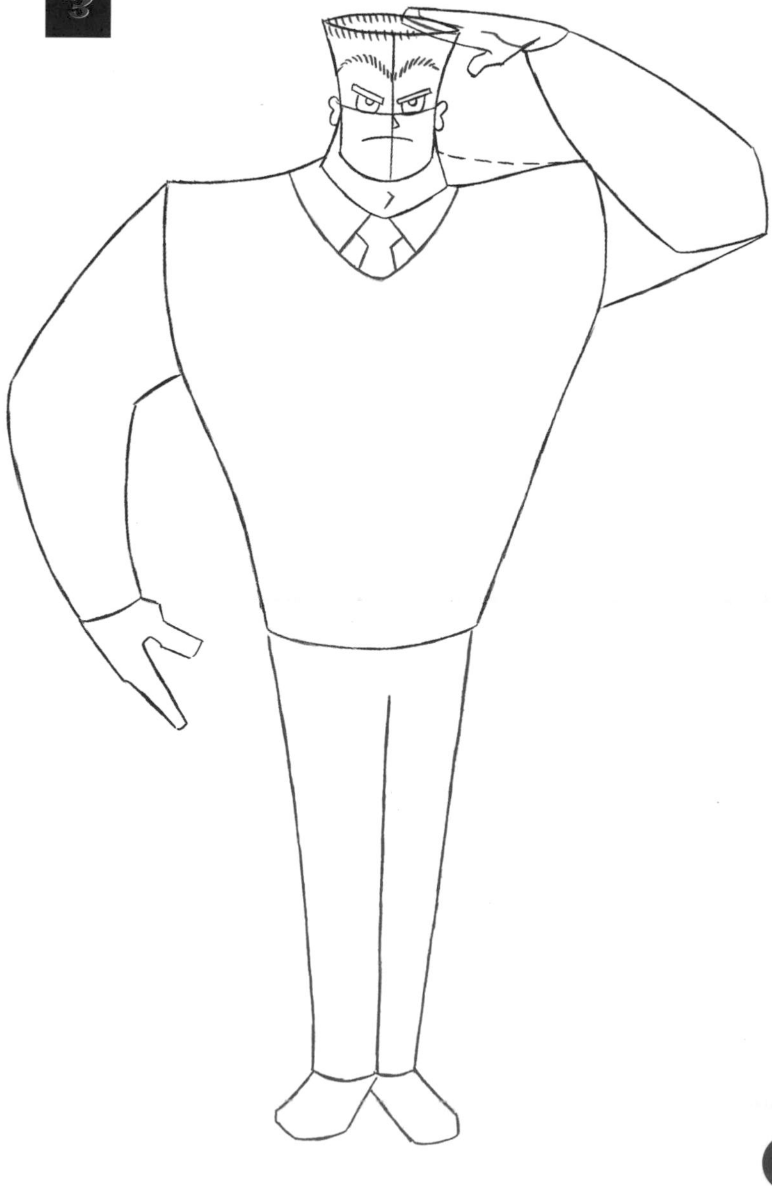

4

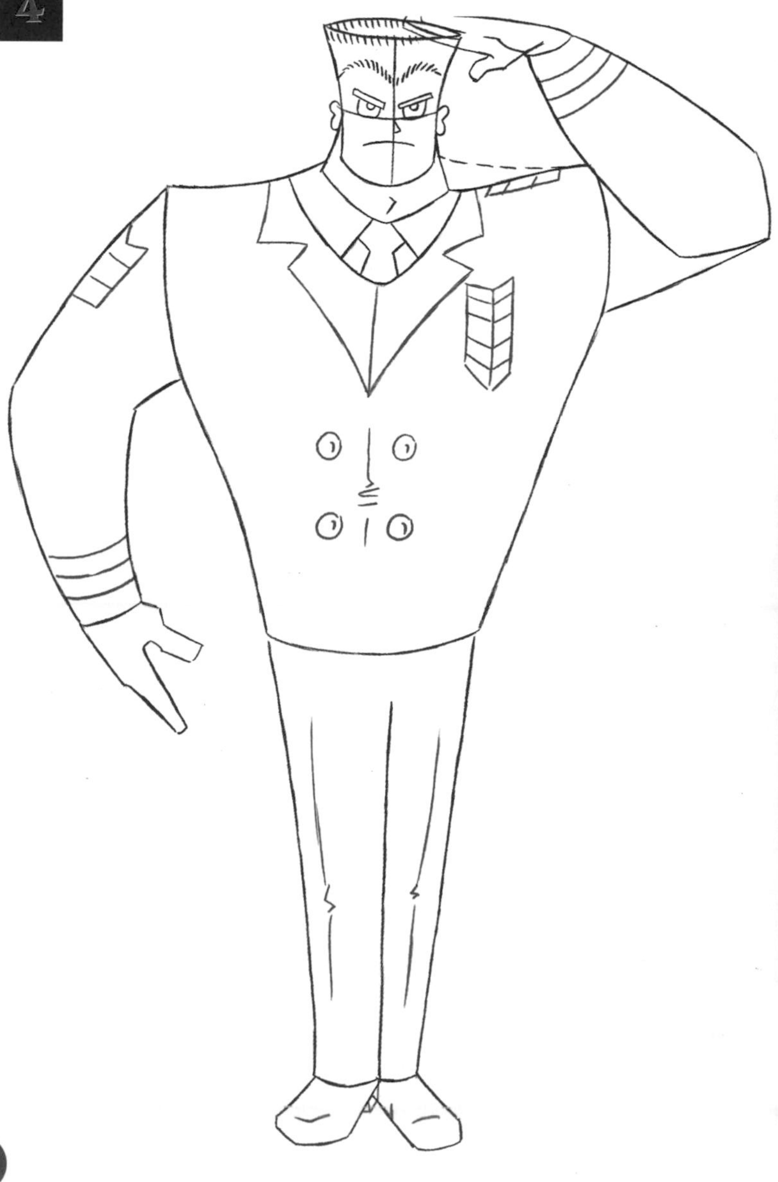

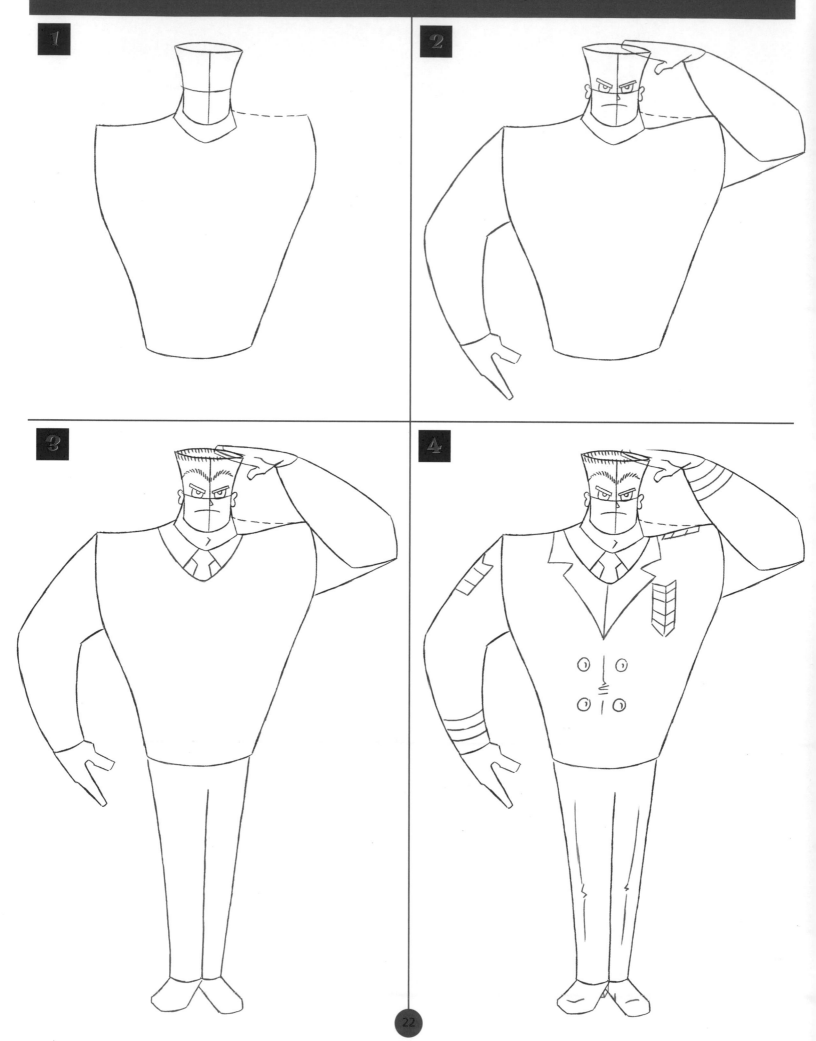

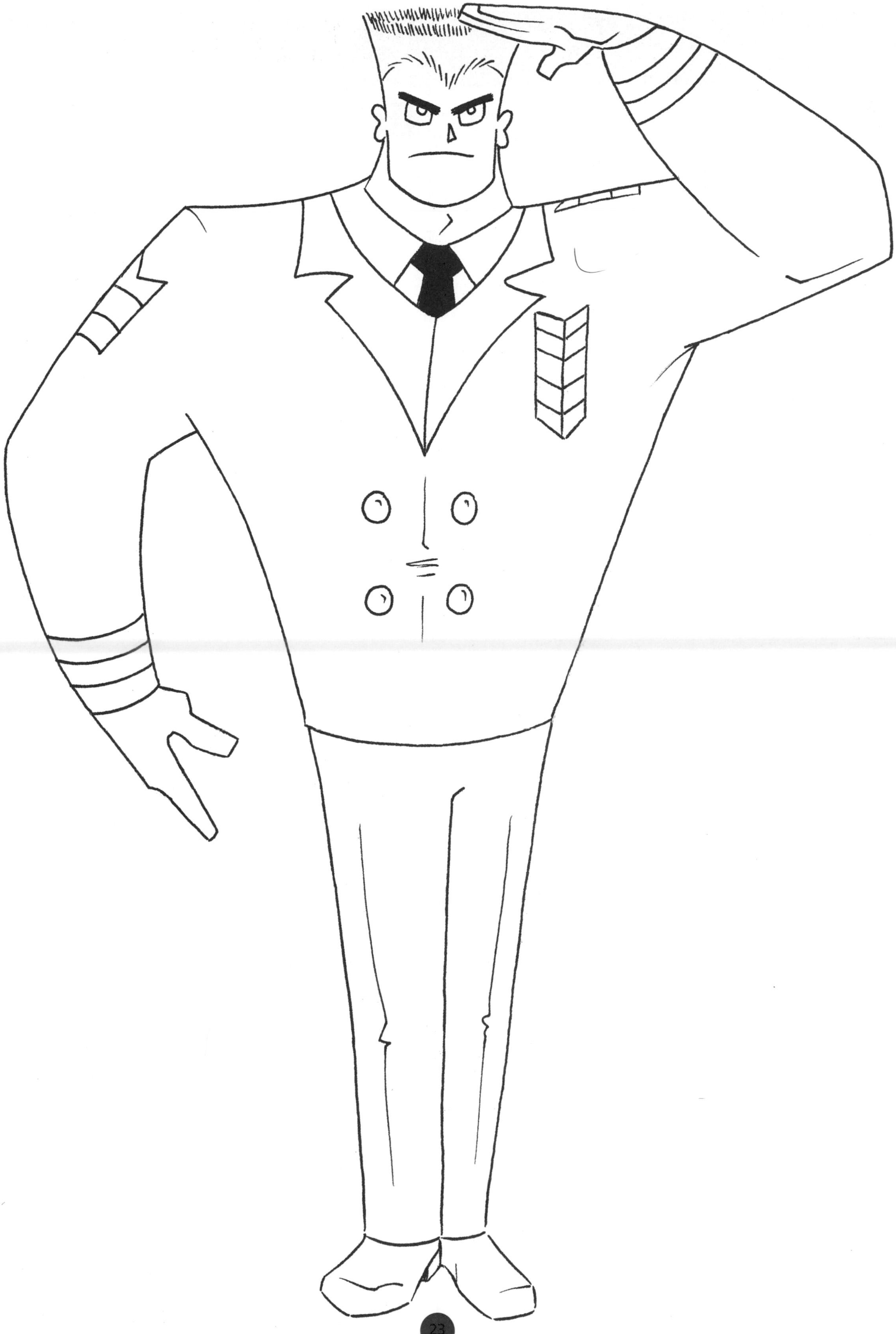

POP-STAR GIRL

1

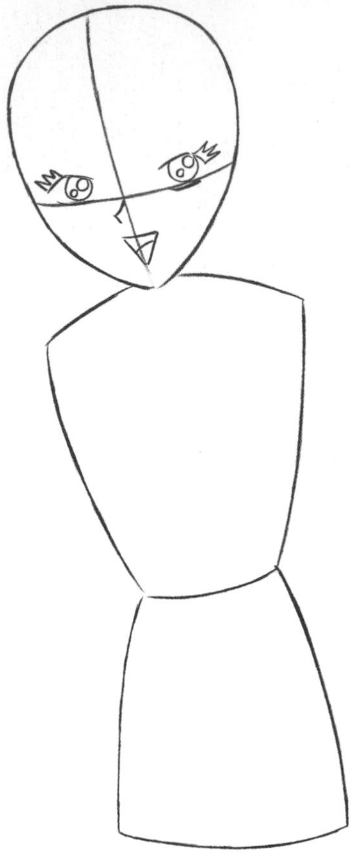

2

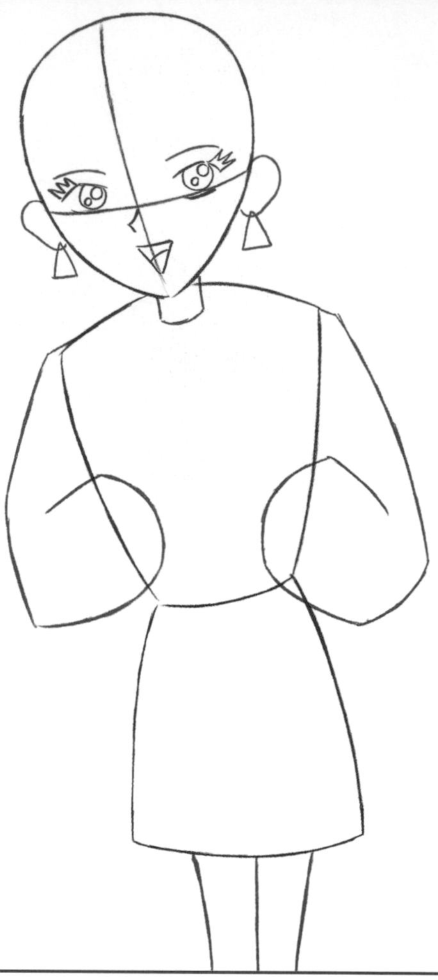

3

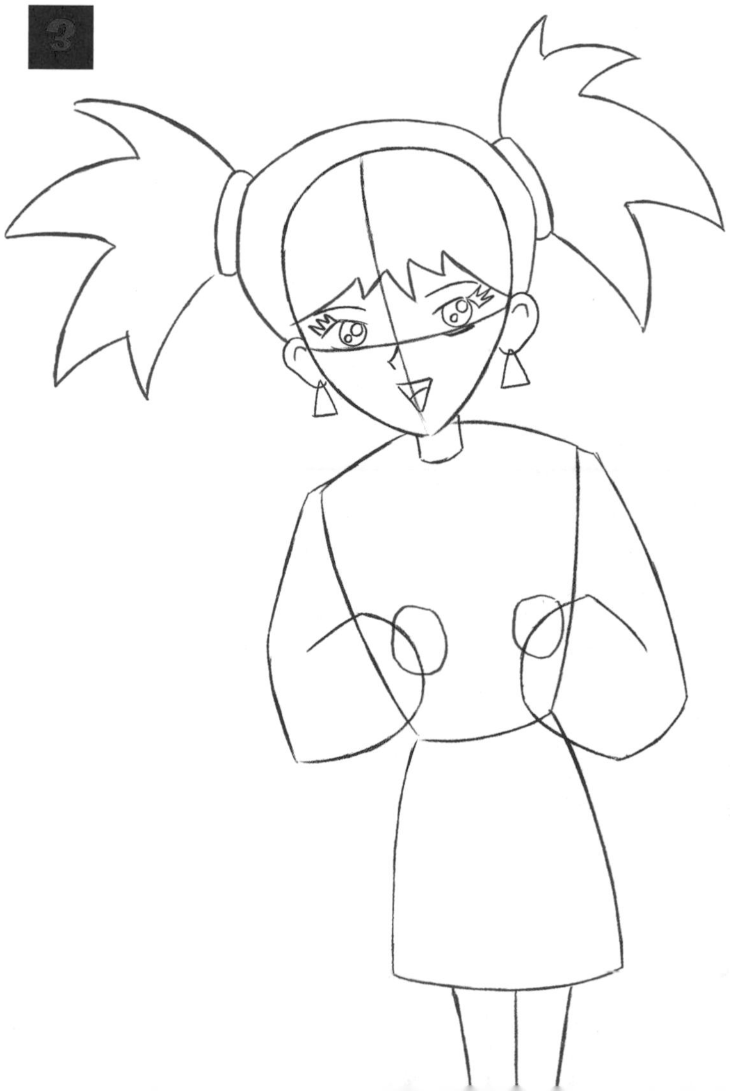

4

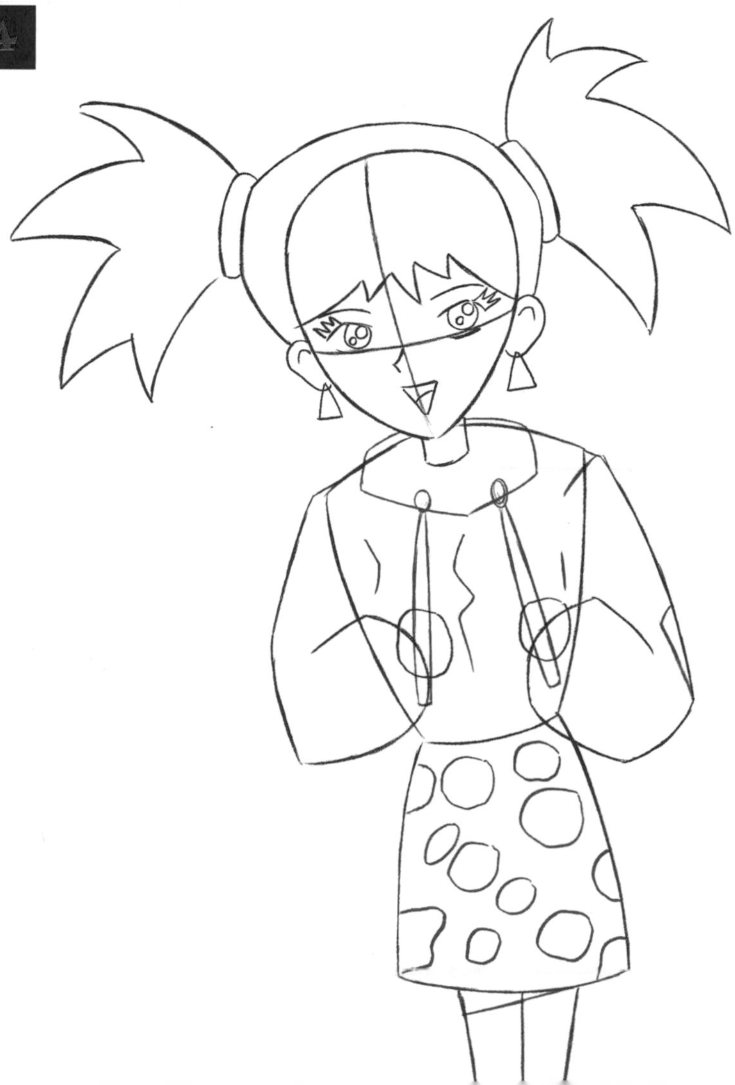

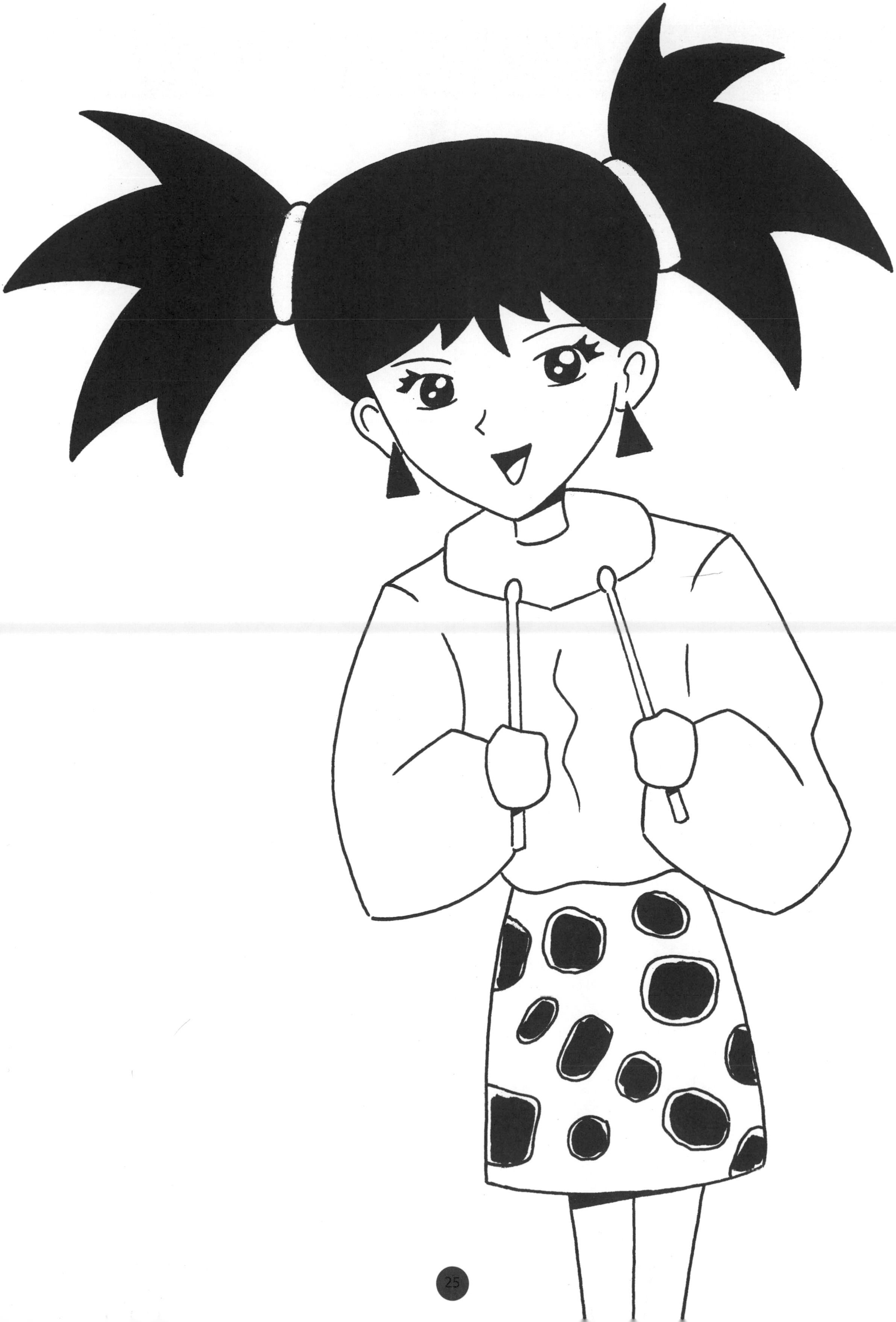

BACKPACK KID

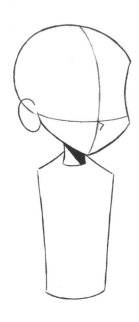

RETRO GIRL

1
2
3
4

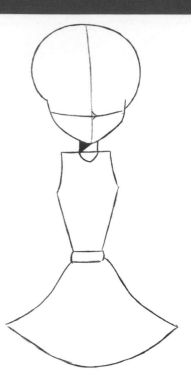

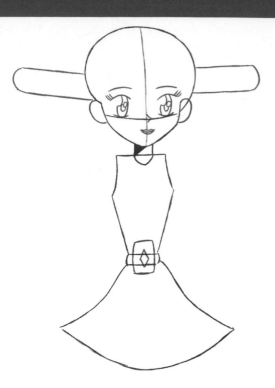

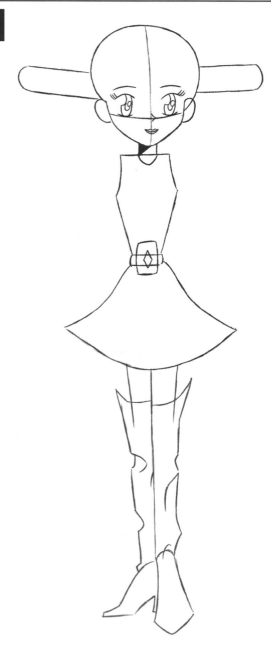

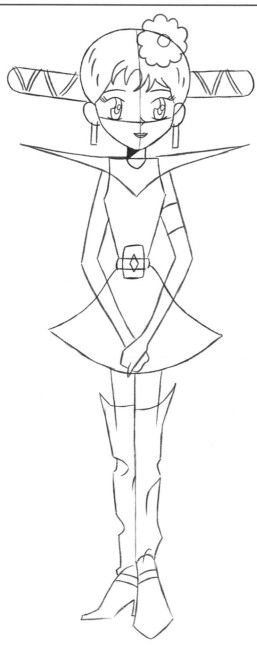

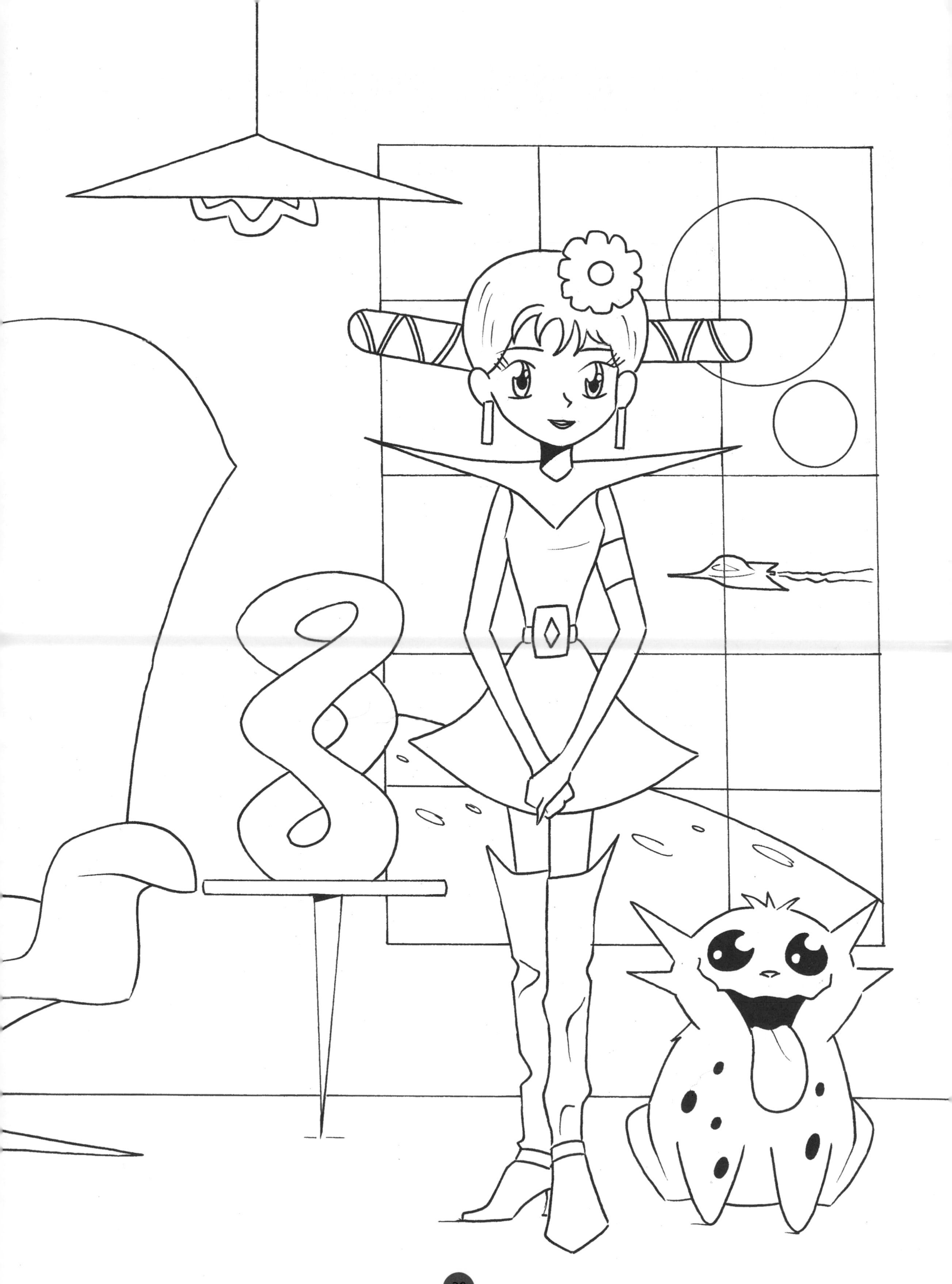

PILOT BOY

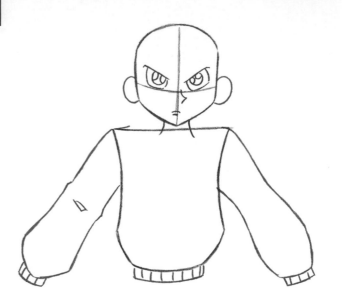

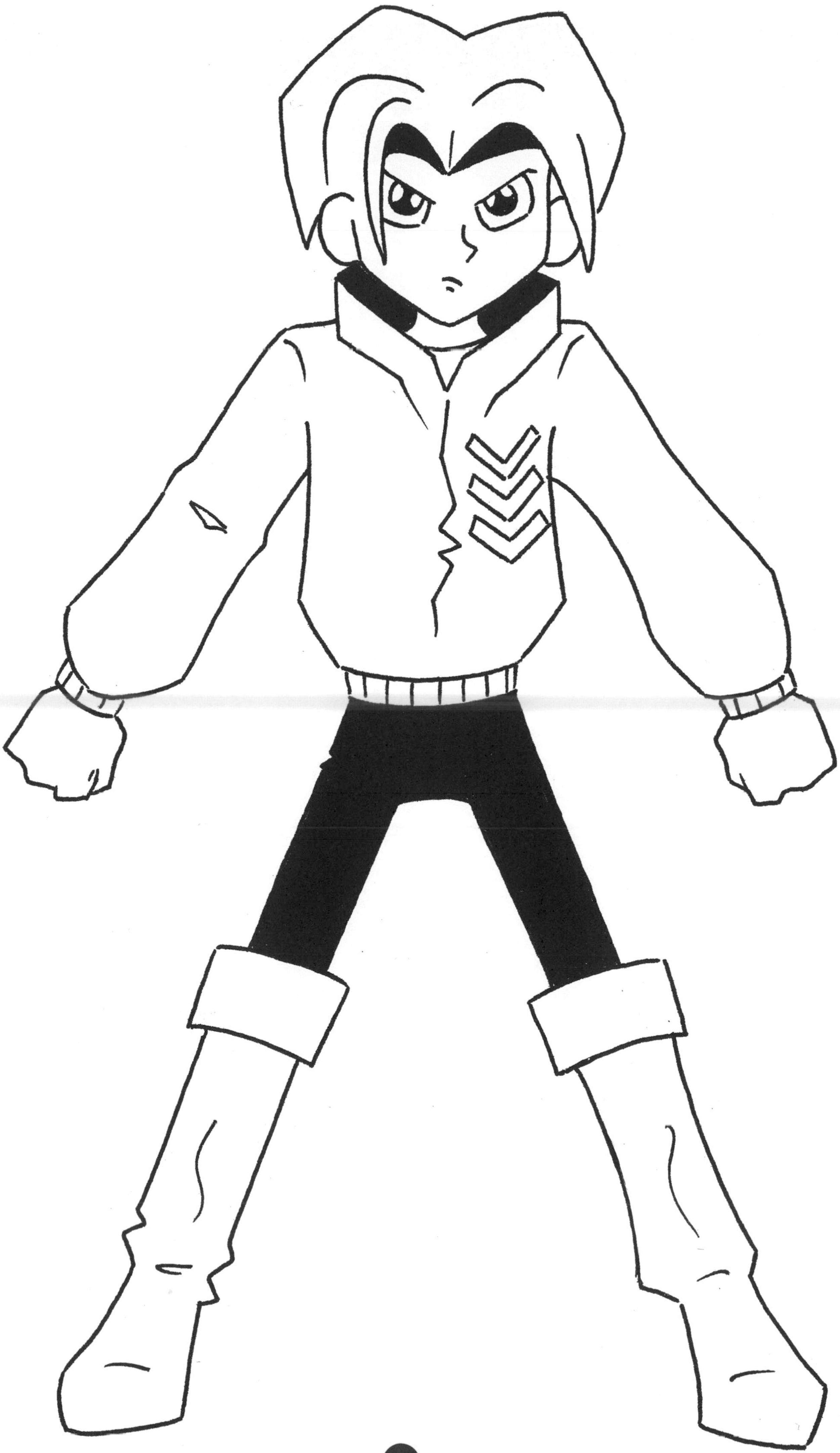

BIG BRAT

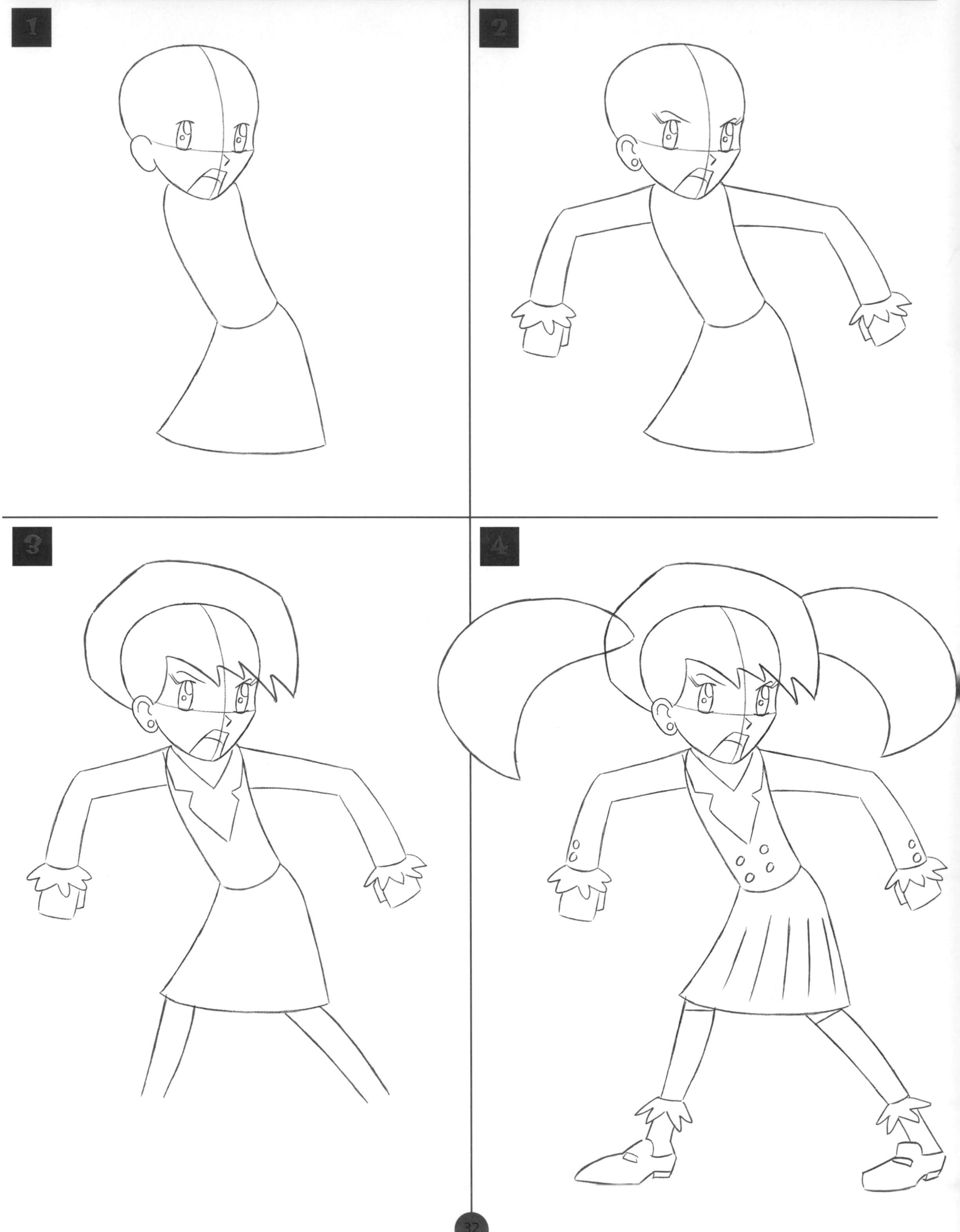
1
2
3
4

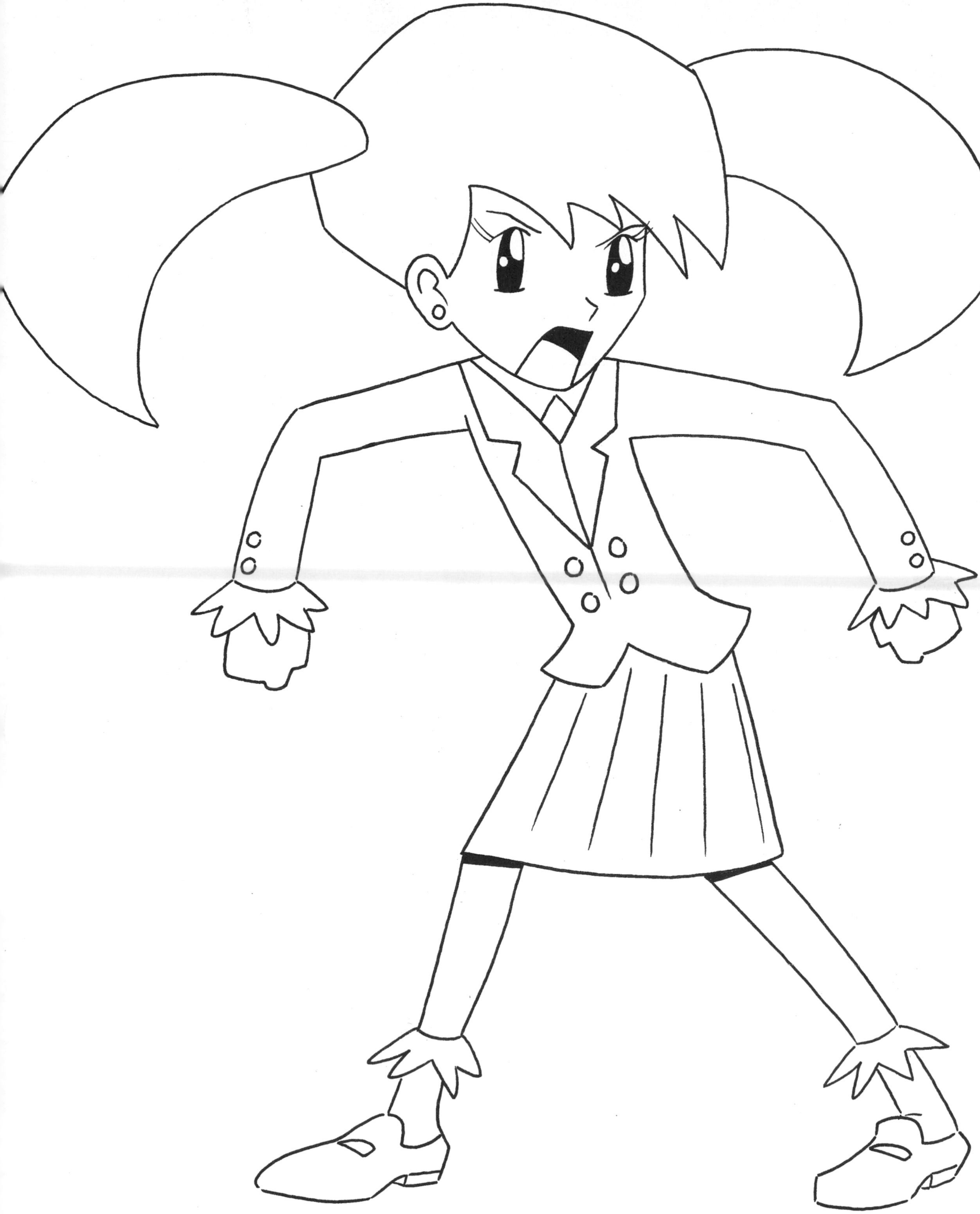

MECHA SOLDIER

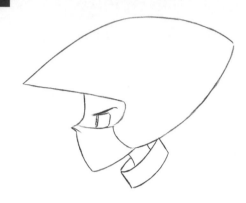

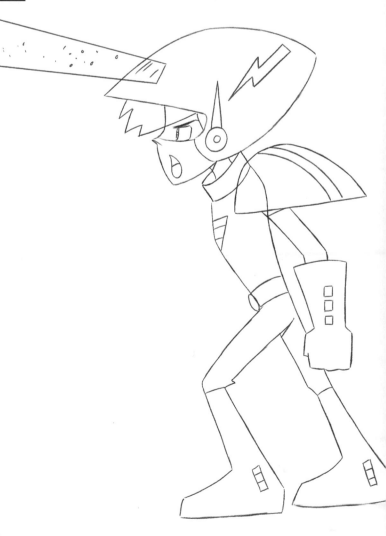

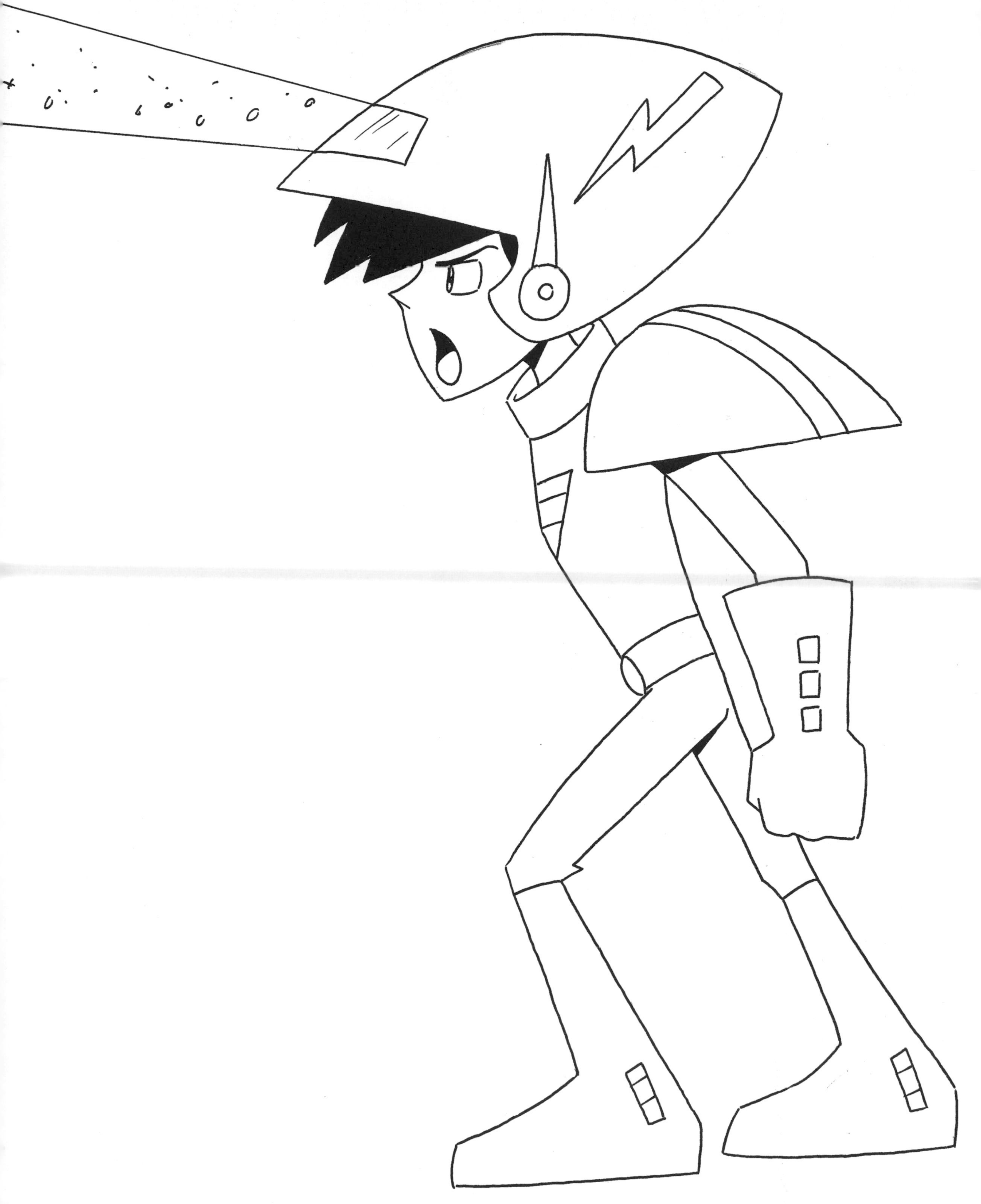

POUNDING PUNCHER

1

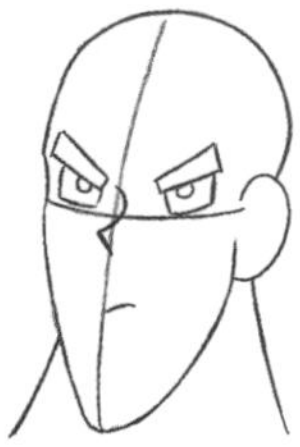

2

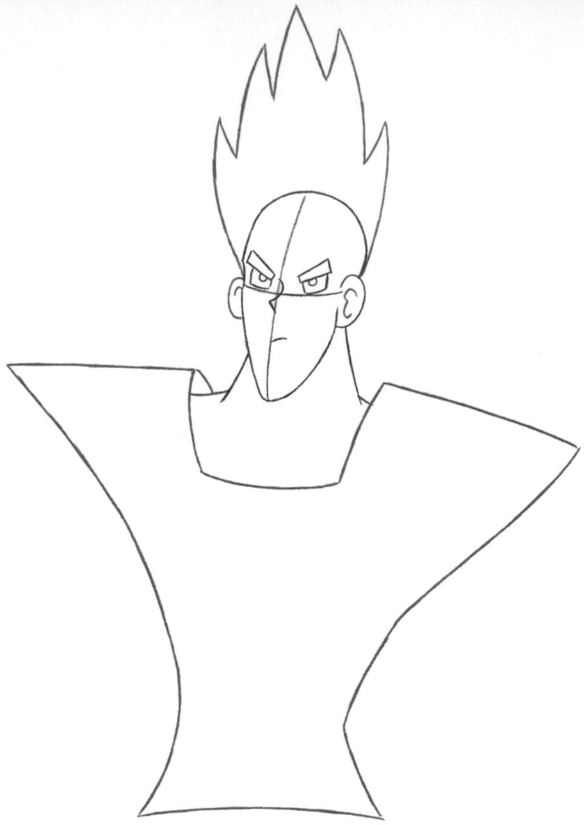

3

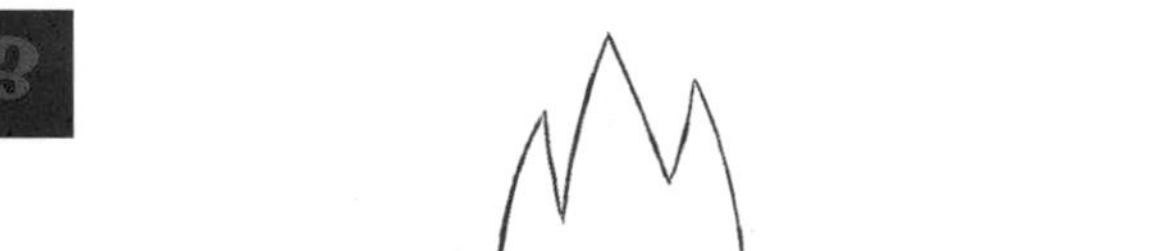

4

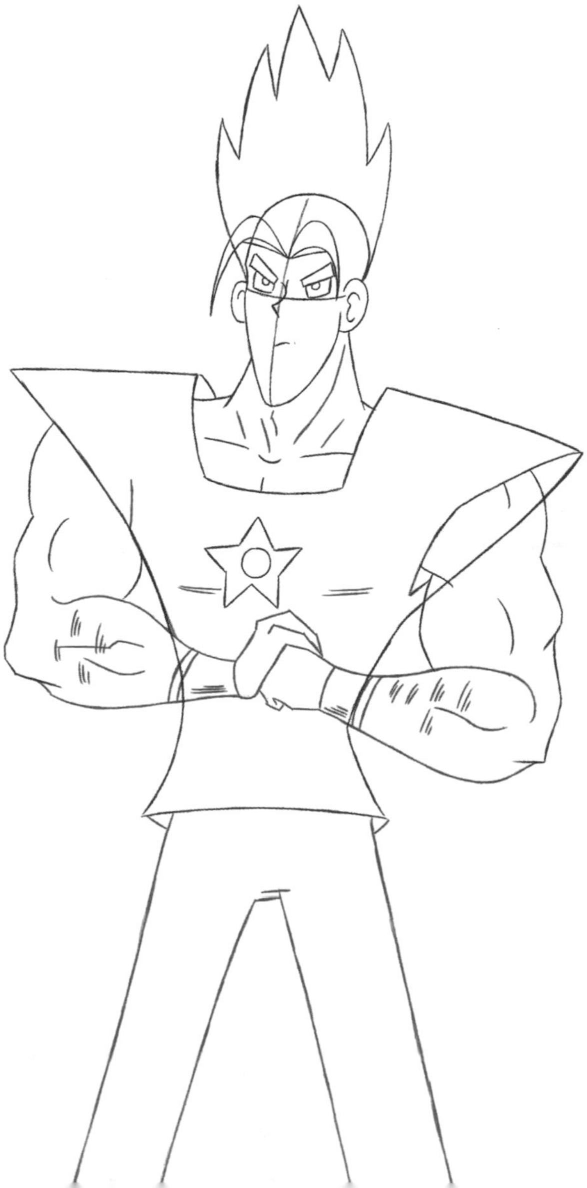

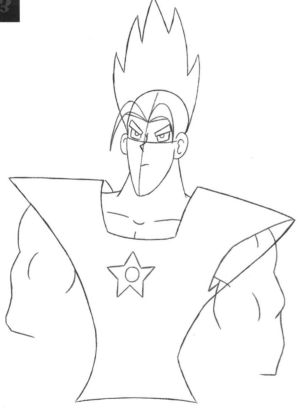

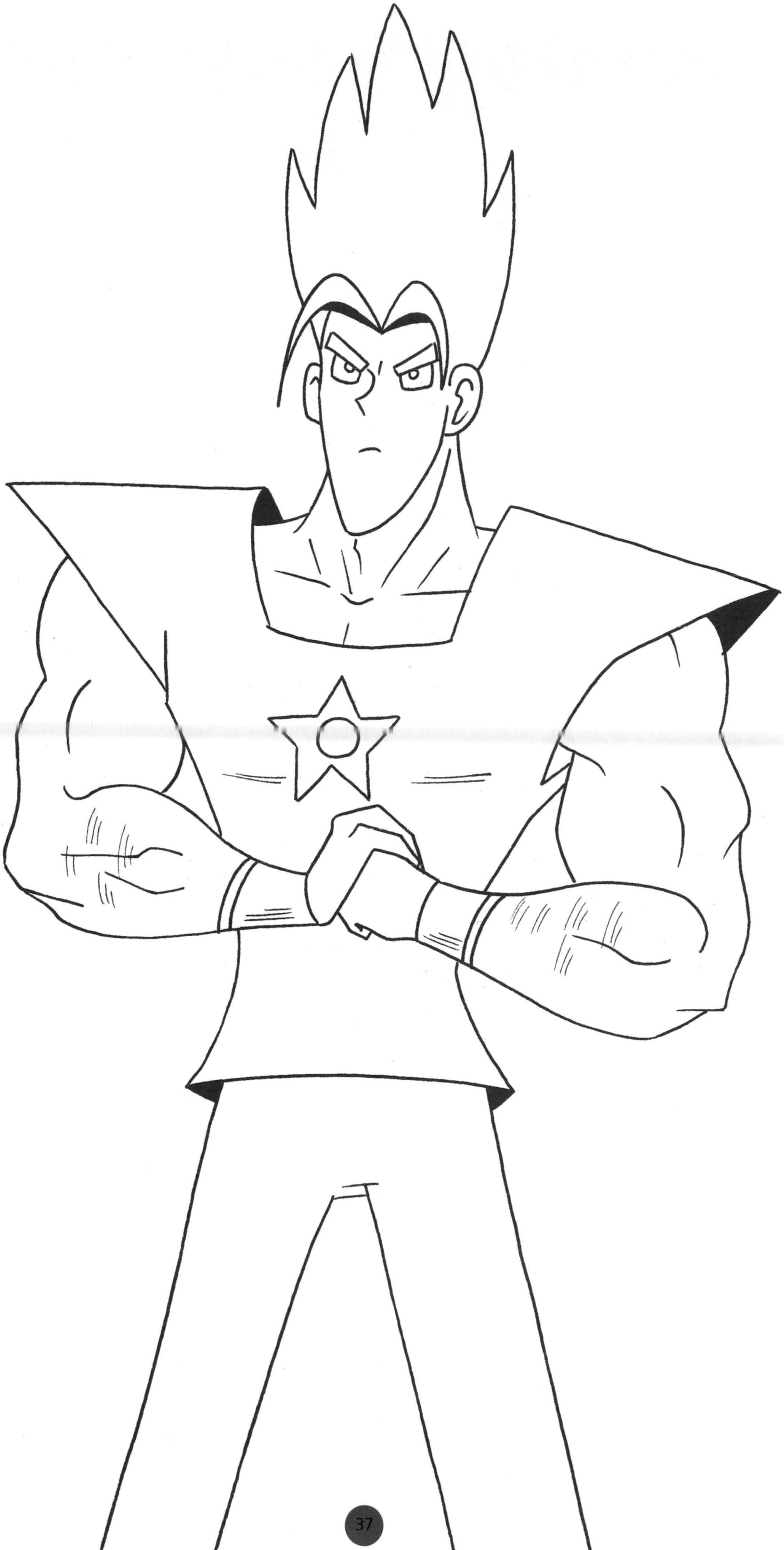

CUDDLY KITTY

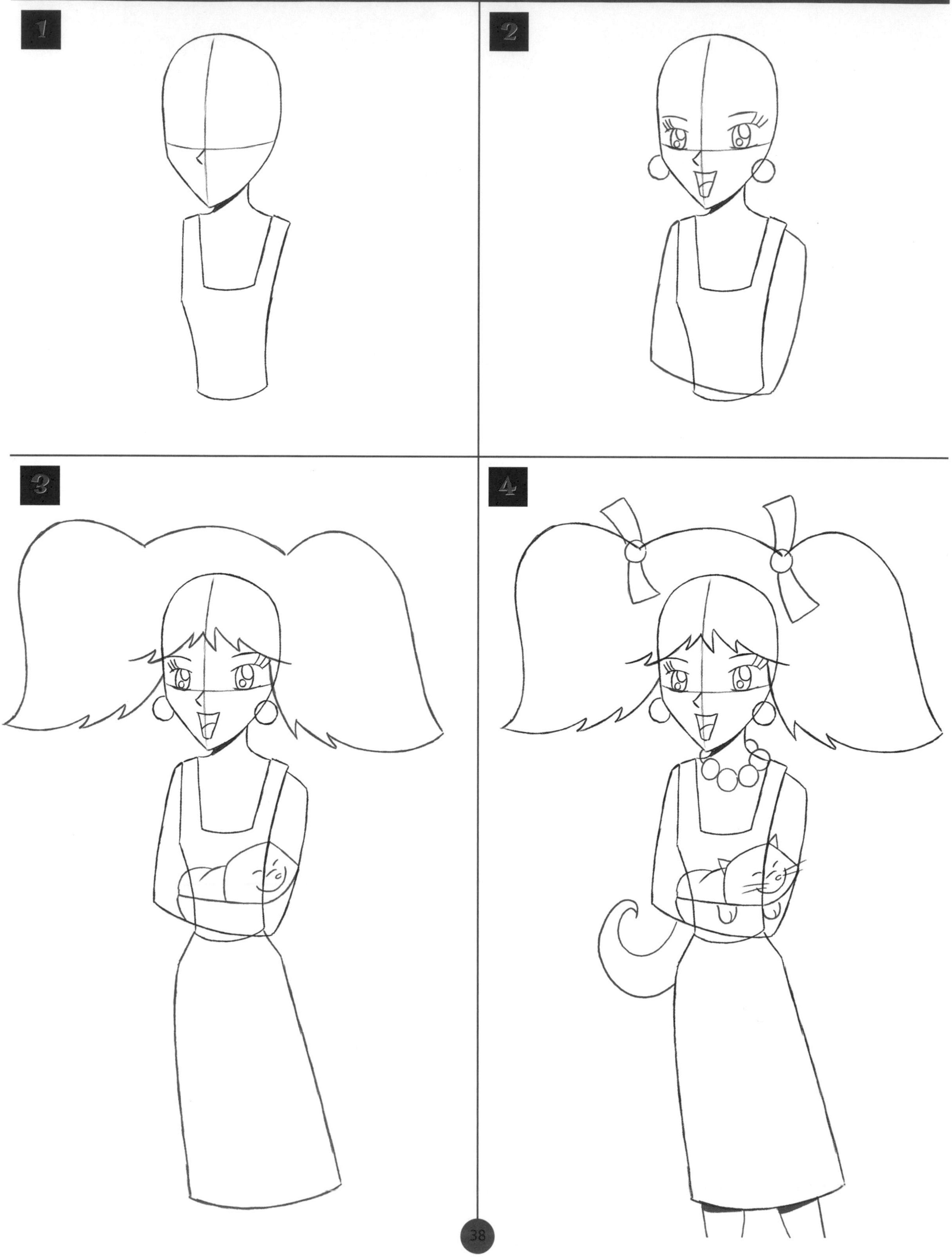
1
2
3
4

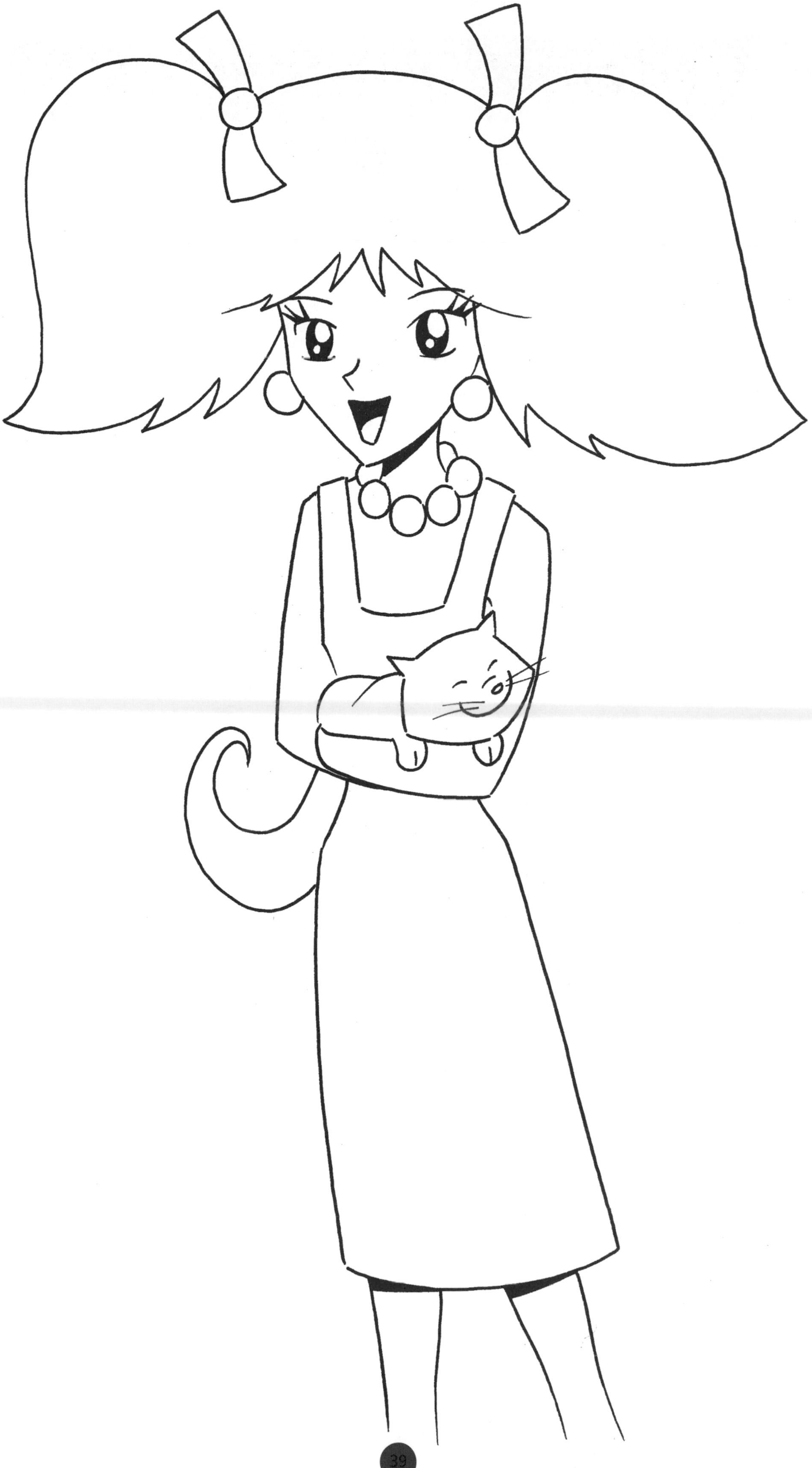

UNDERCOVER AGENT

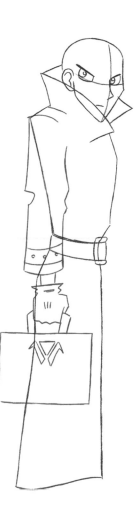

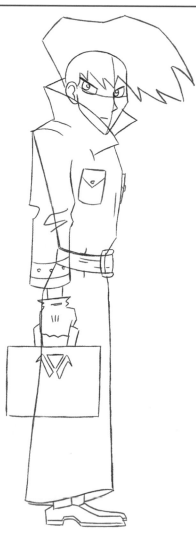

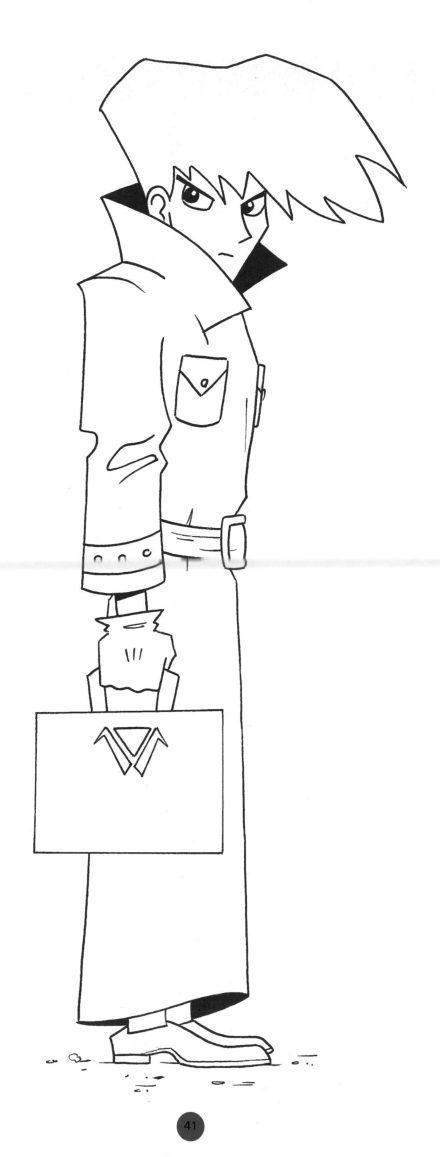

FRIENDLY GIRL

1

2

3

4

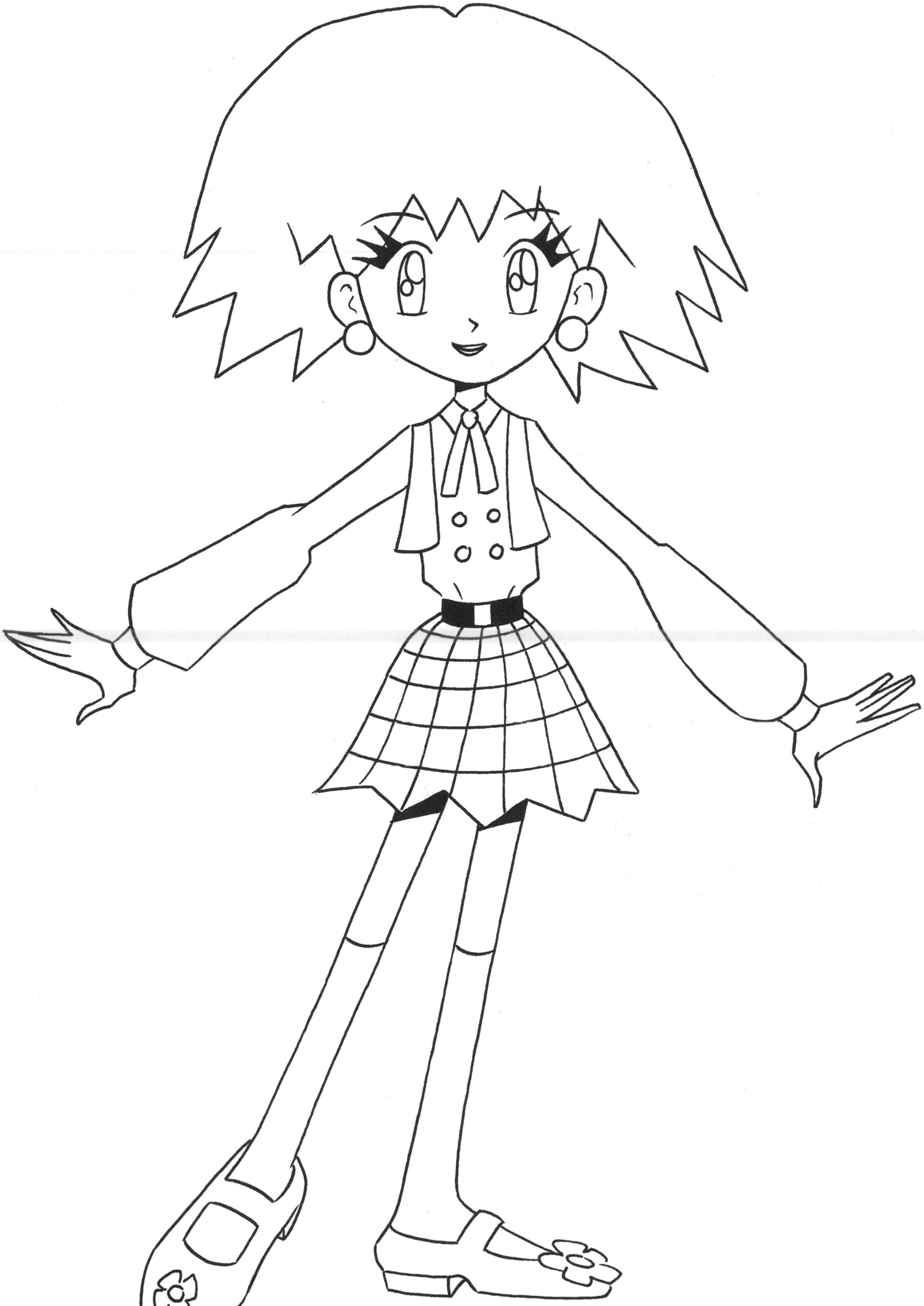

SHADY LADY

1

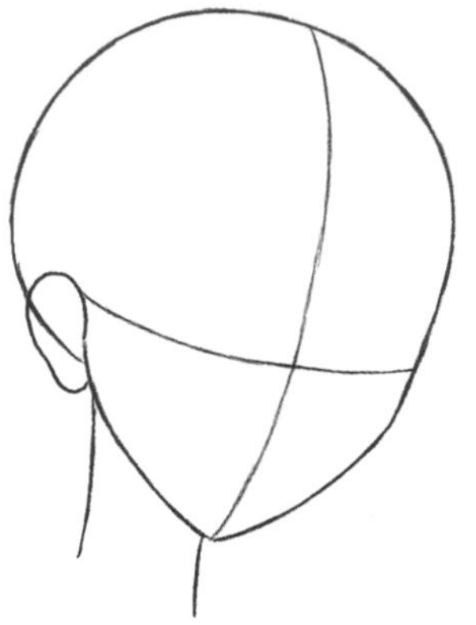

2

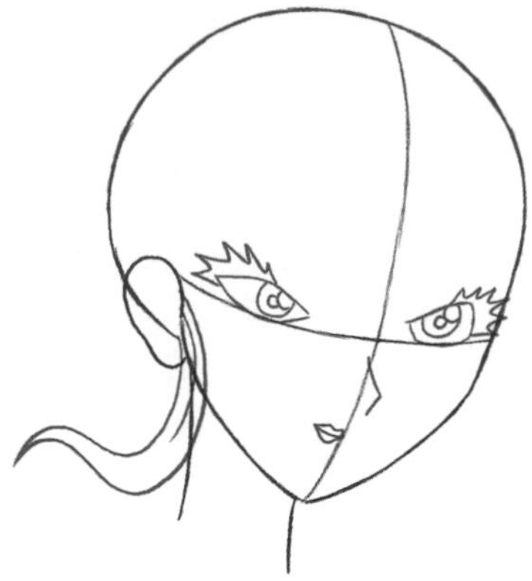

3

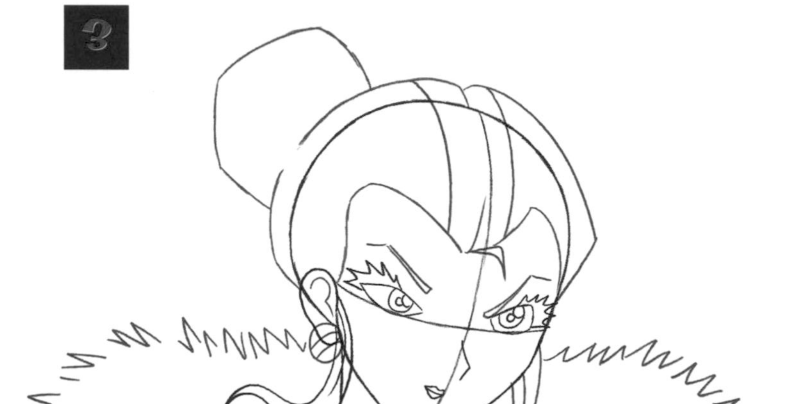

4

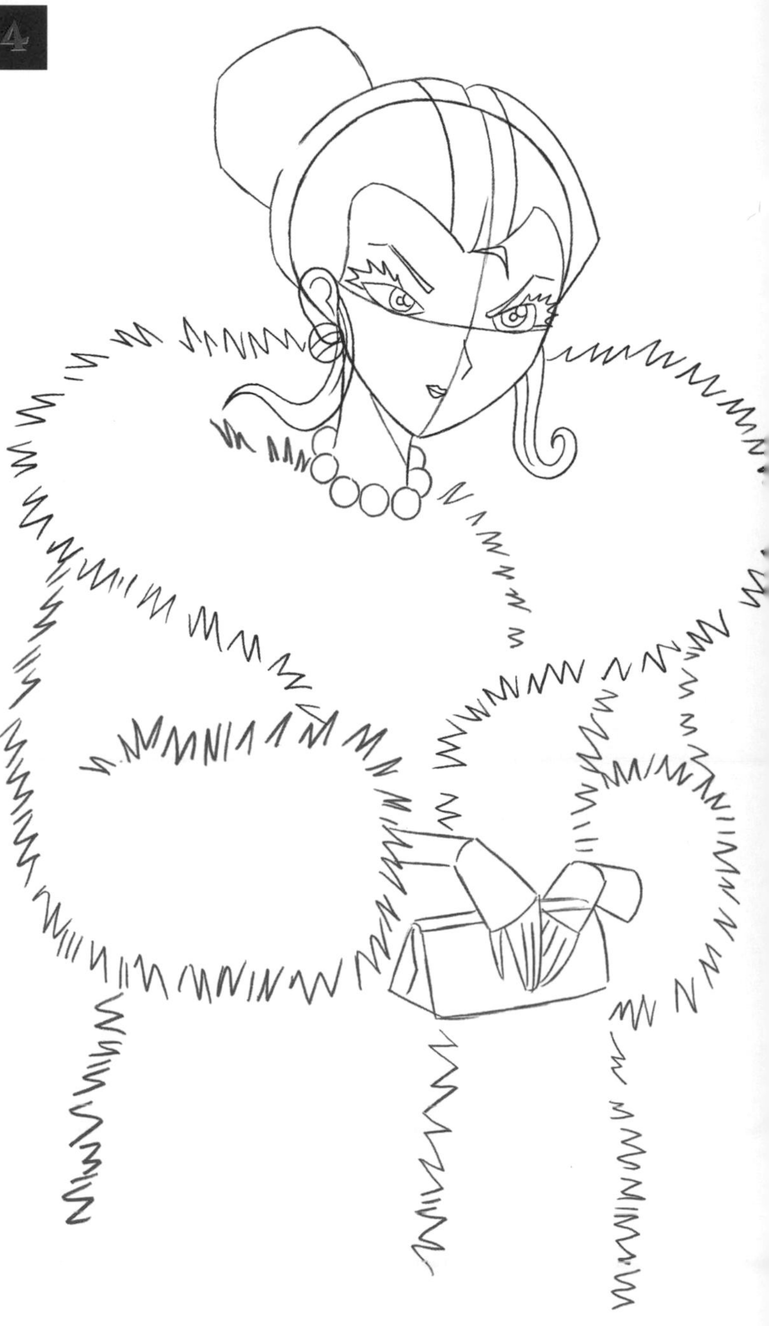

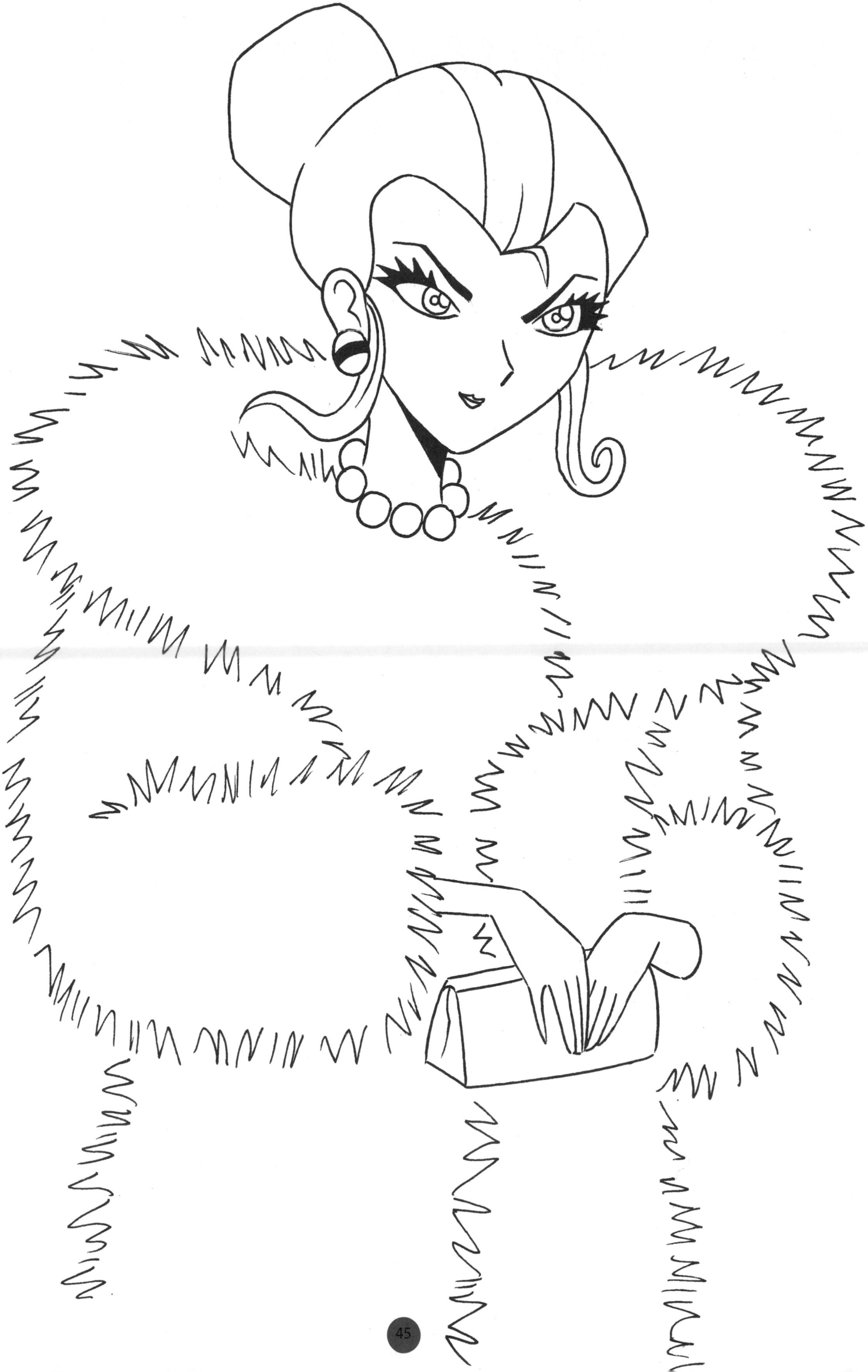

MEAN TEEN

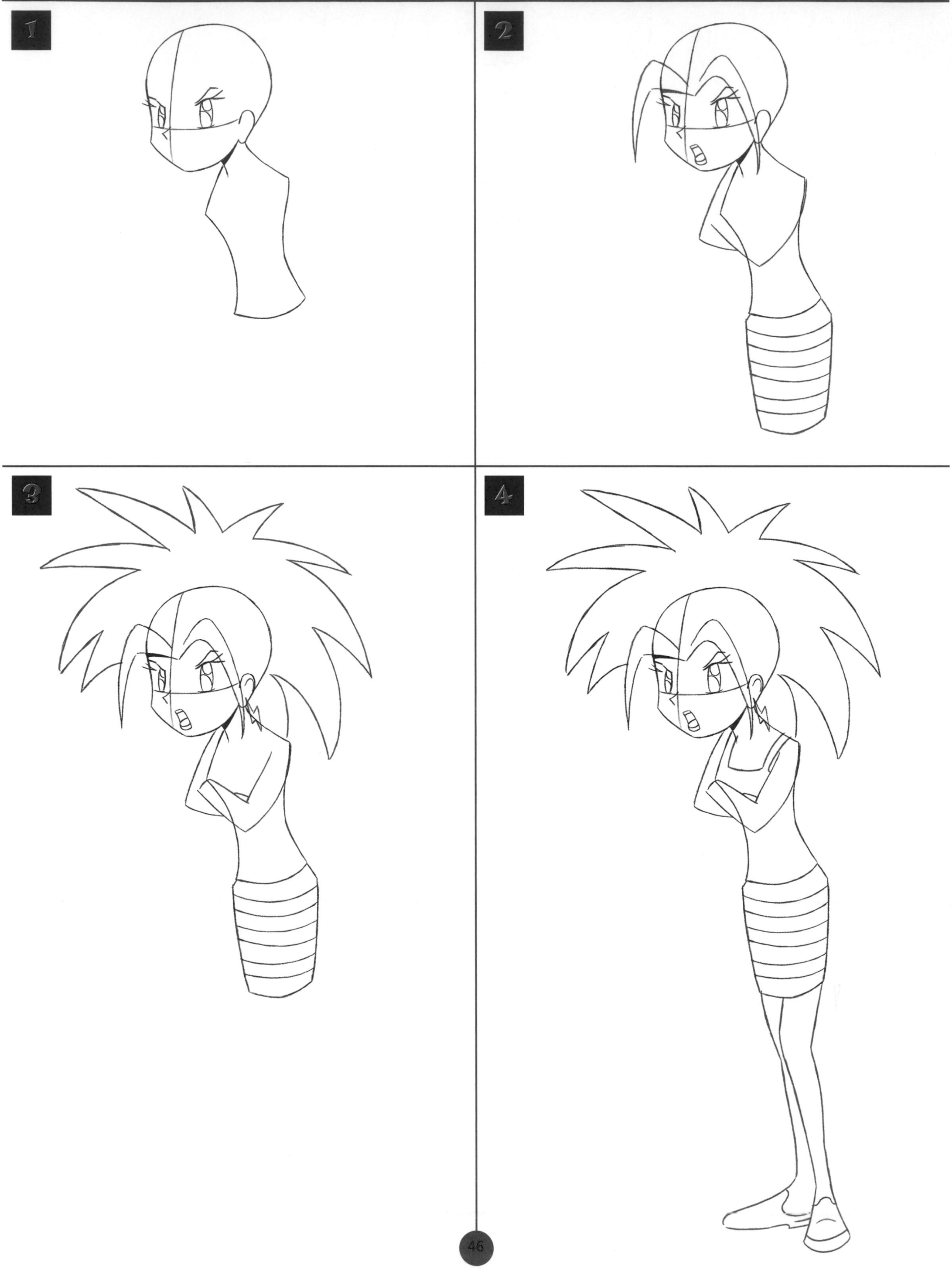
1
2
3
4

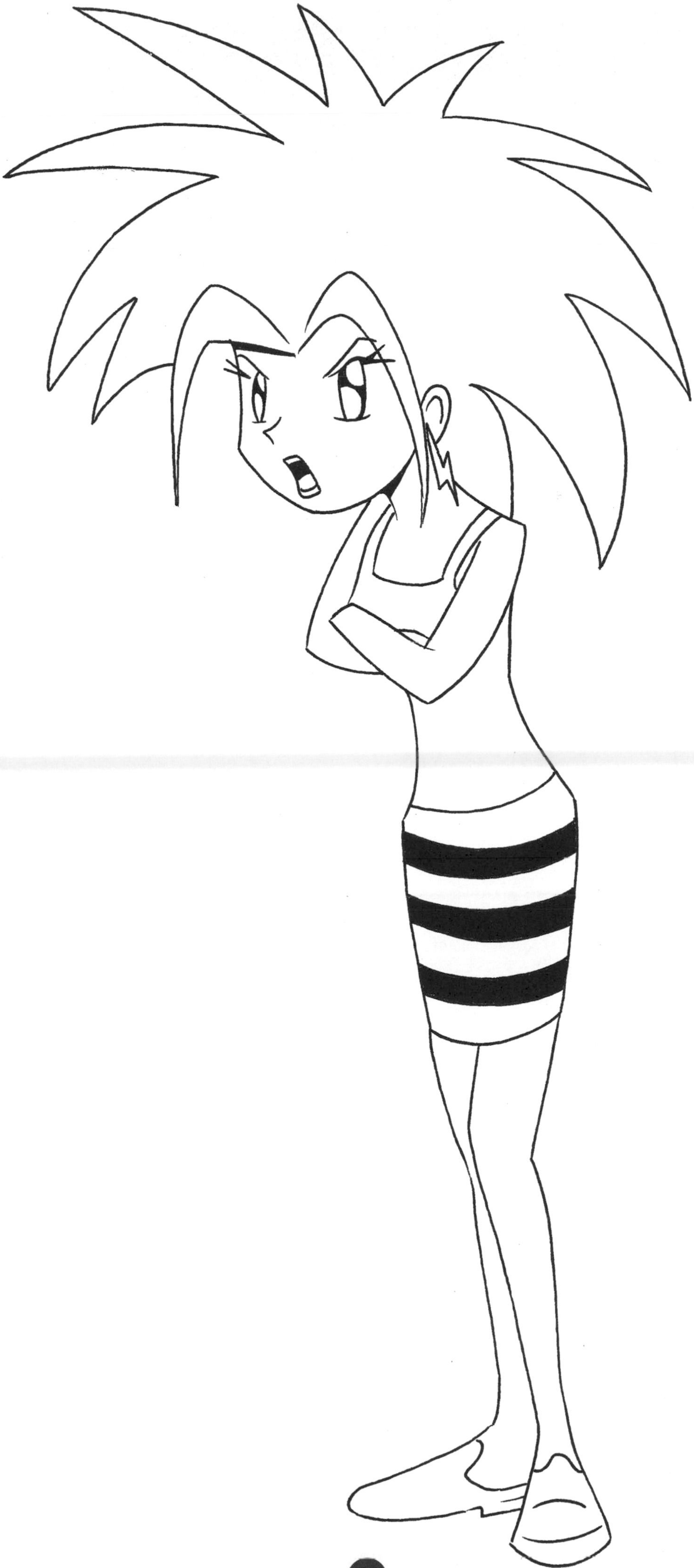

MR. COOL

1

2

3

4

ZEBRA PANTS

1

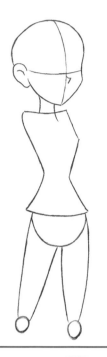

2

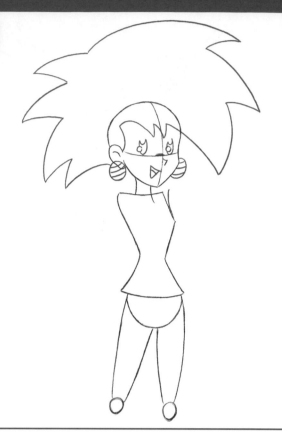

3

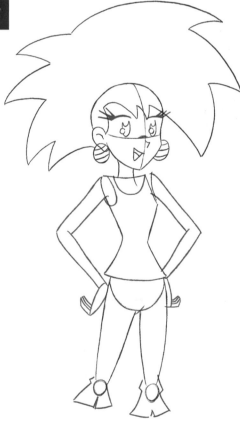

4

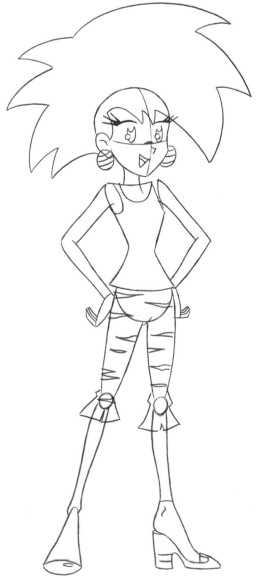

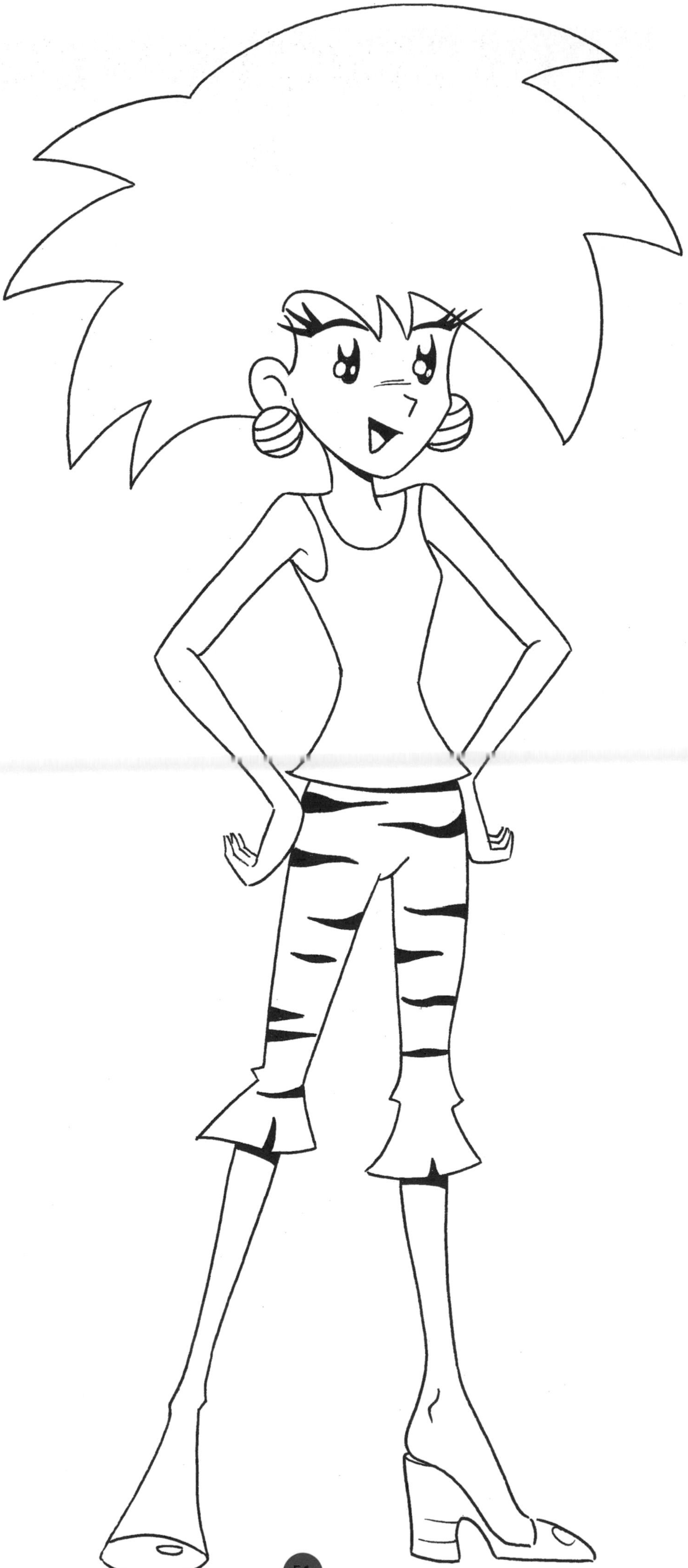

PULSING POWER

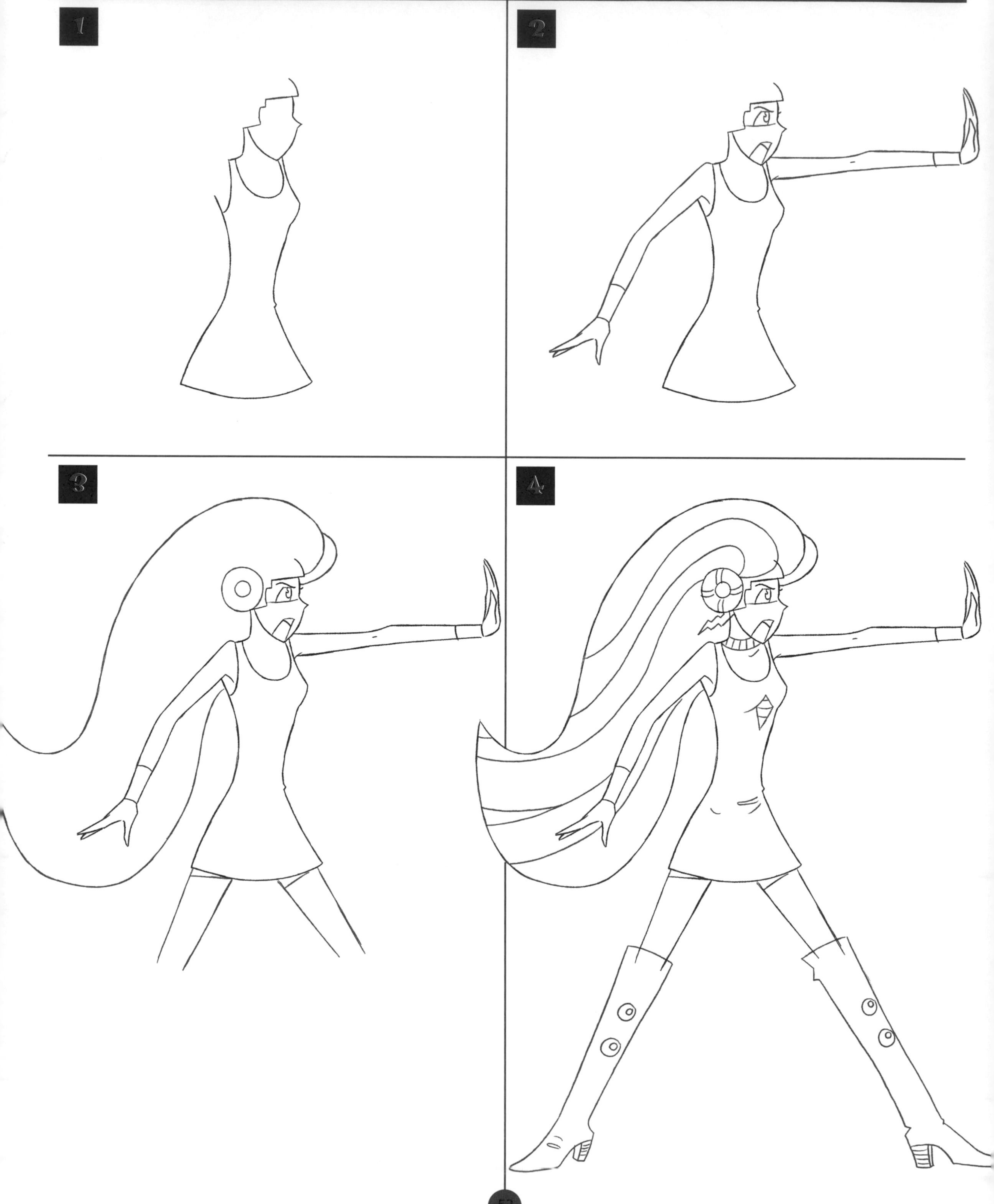
1
2
3
4

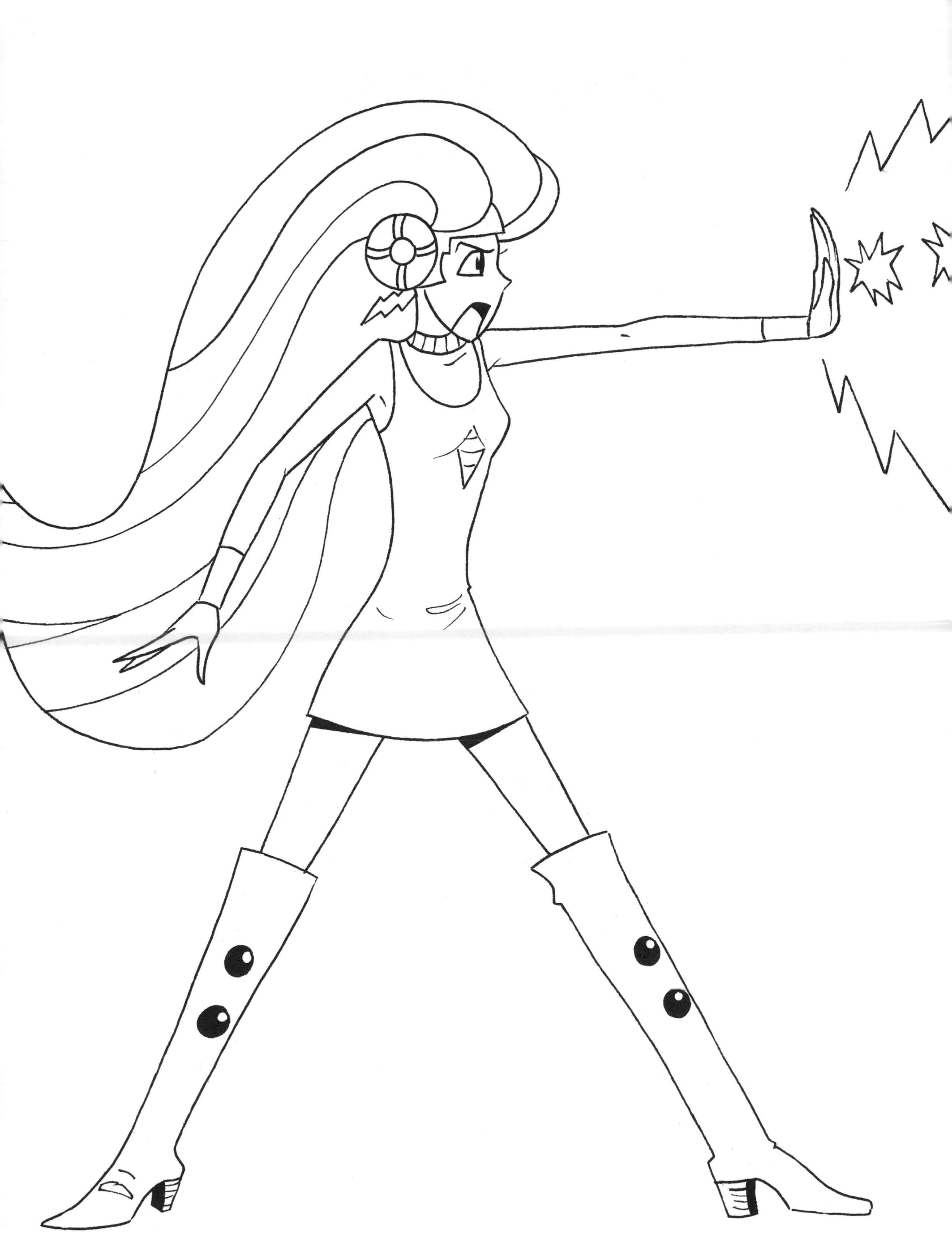

EVIL WARLOCK

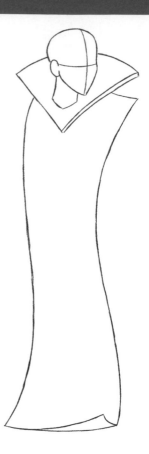

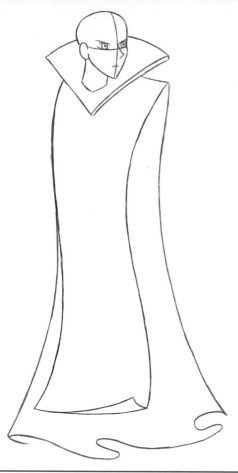

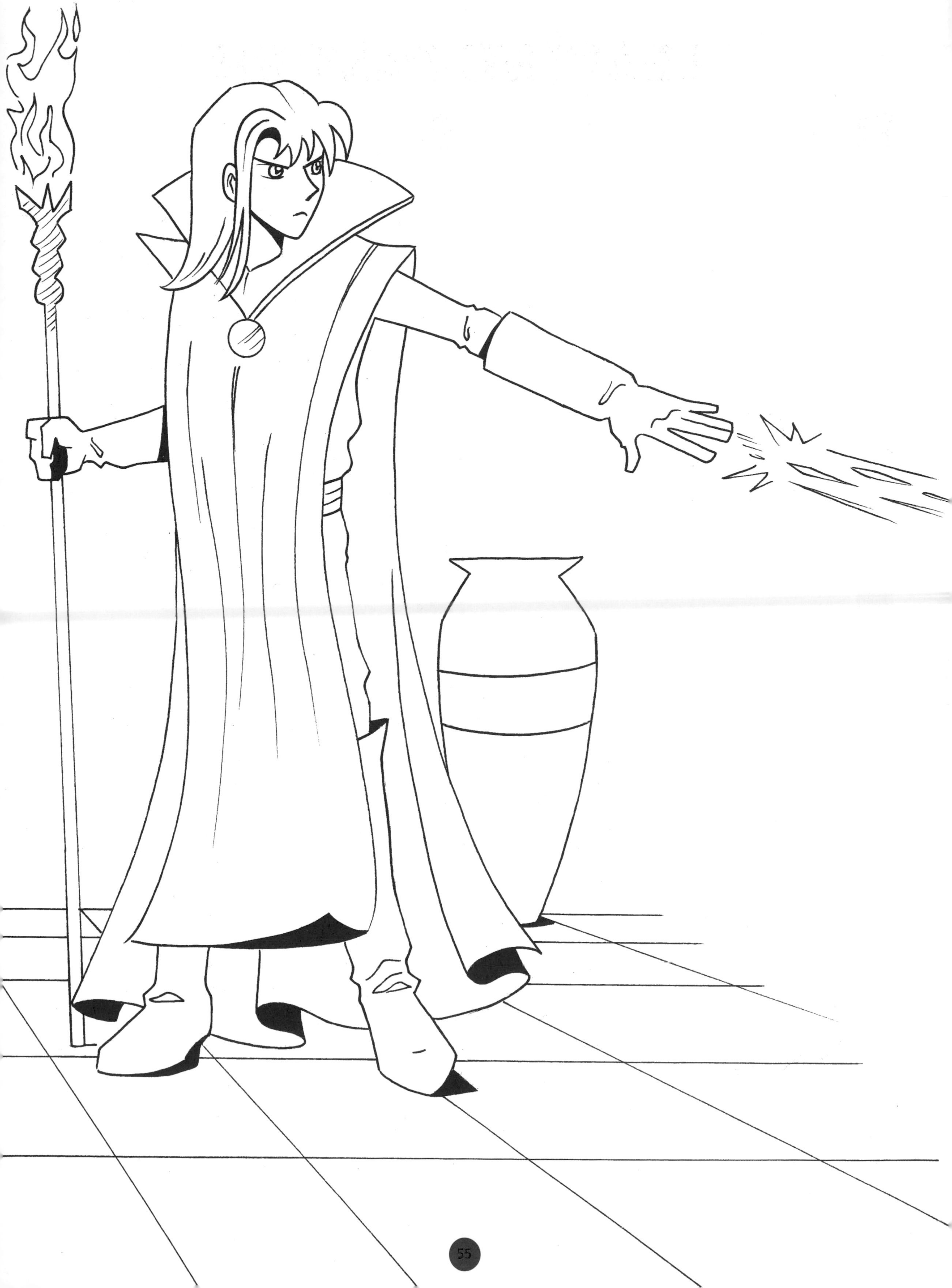

LEAPING DANCER

1

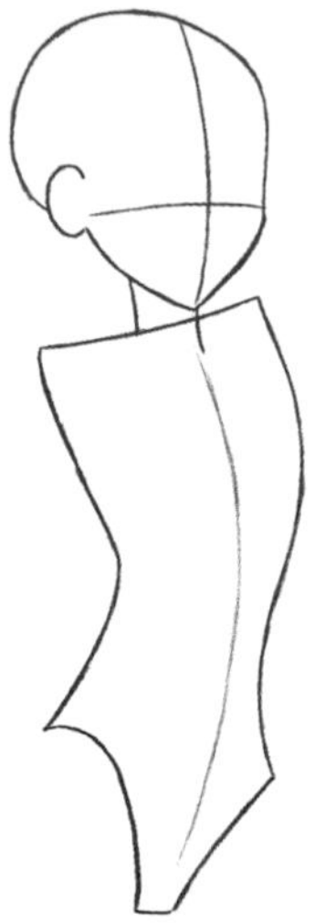

2

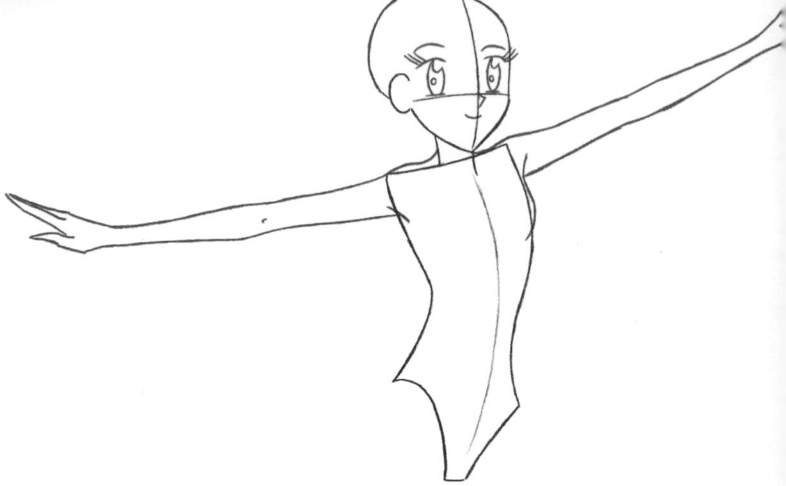

3

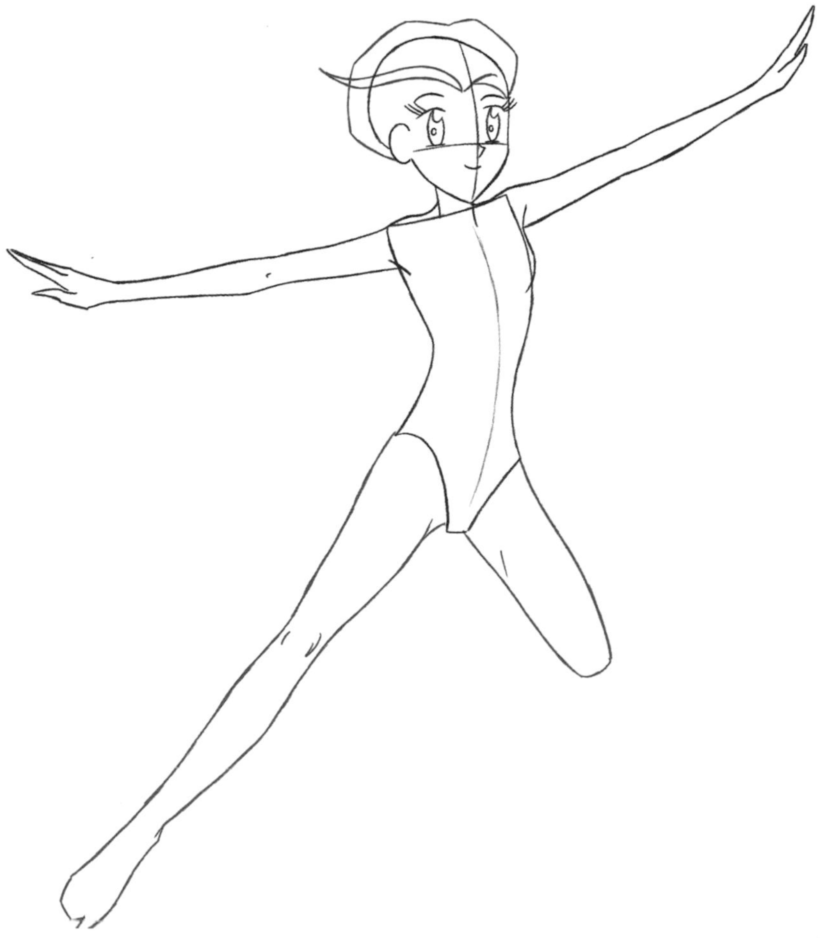

4

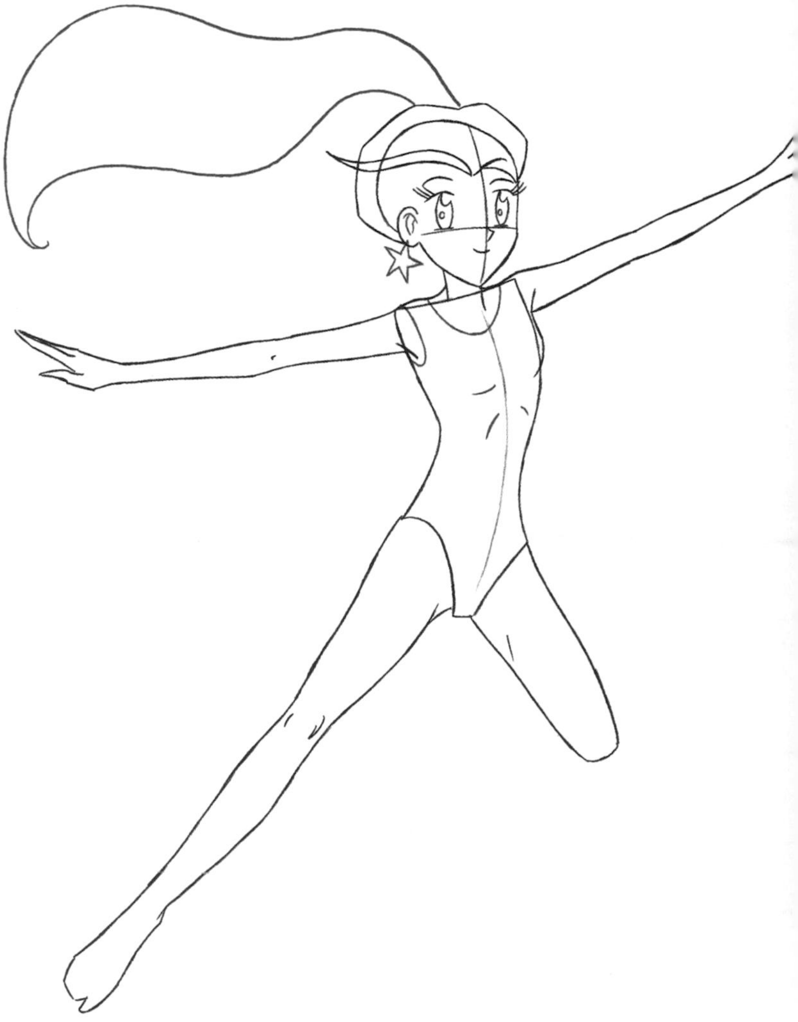

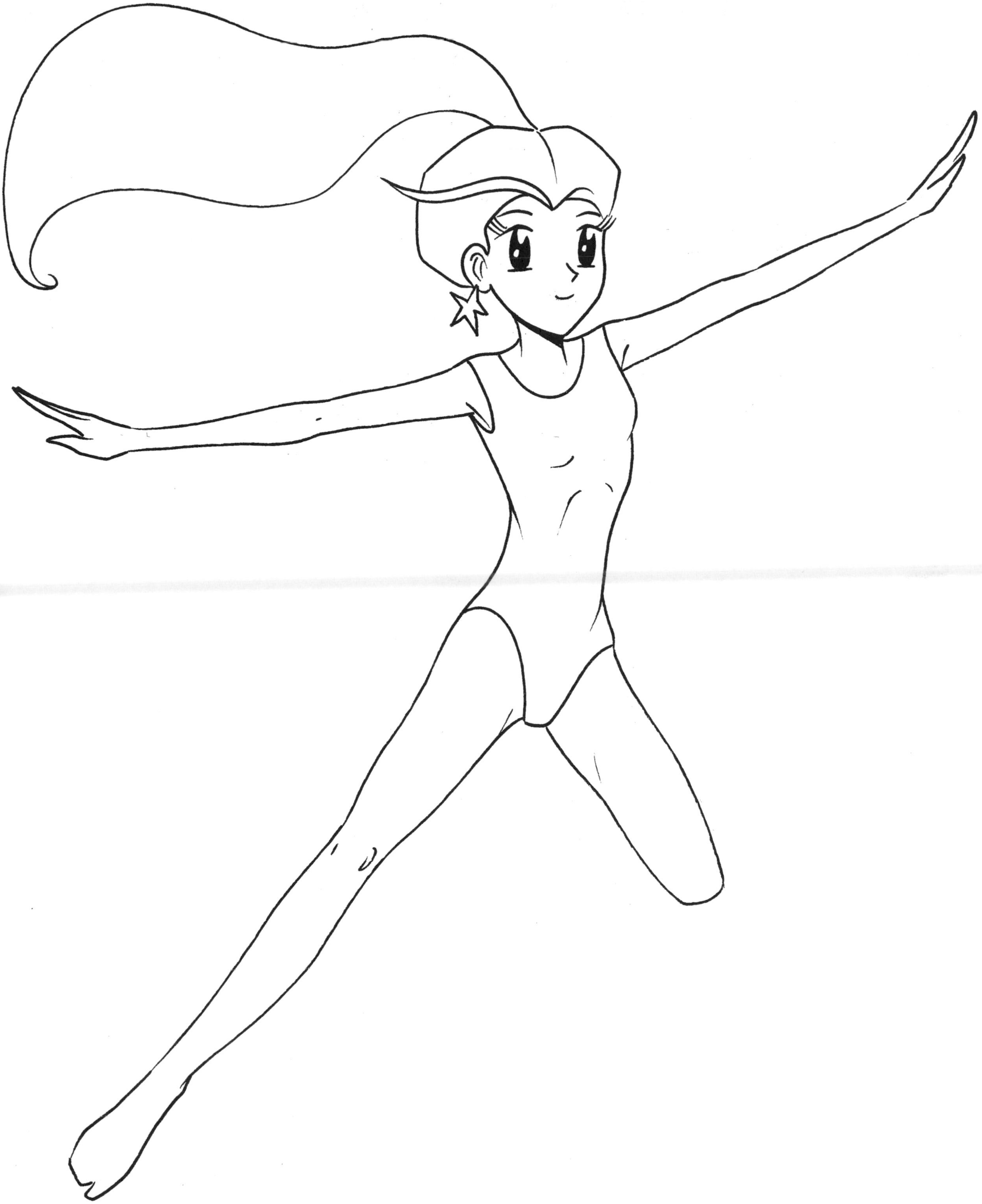

BIG CRUSH

1

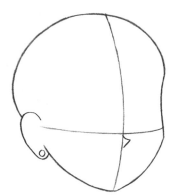

2

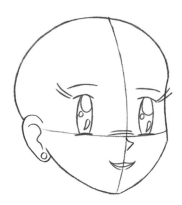

3

4

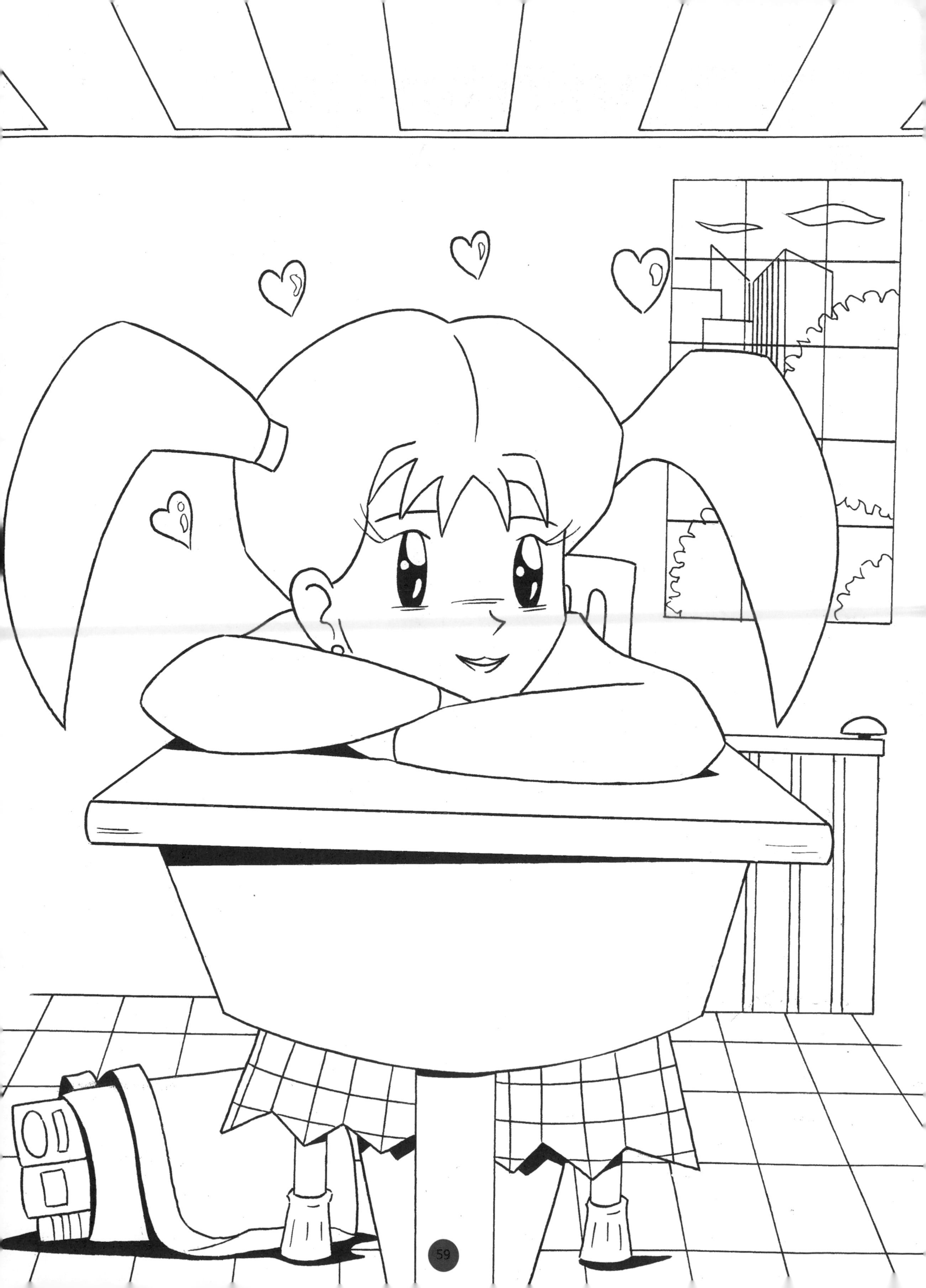

METEOR GIRL

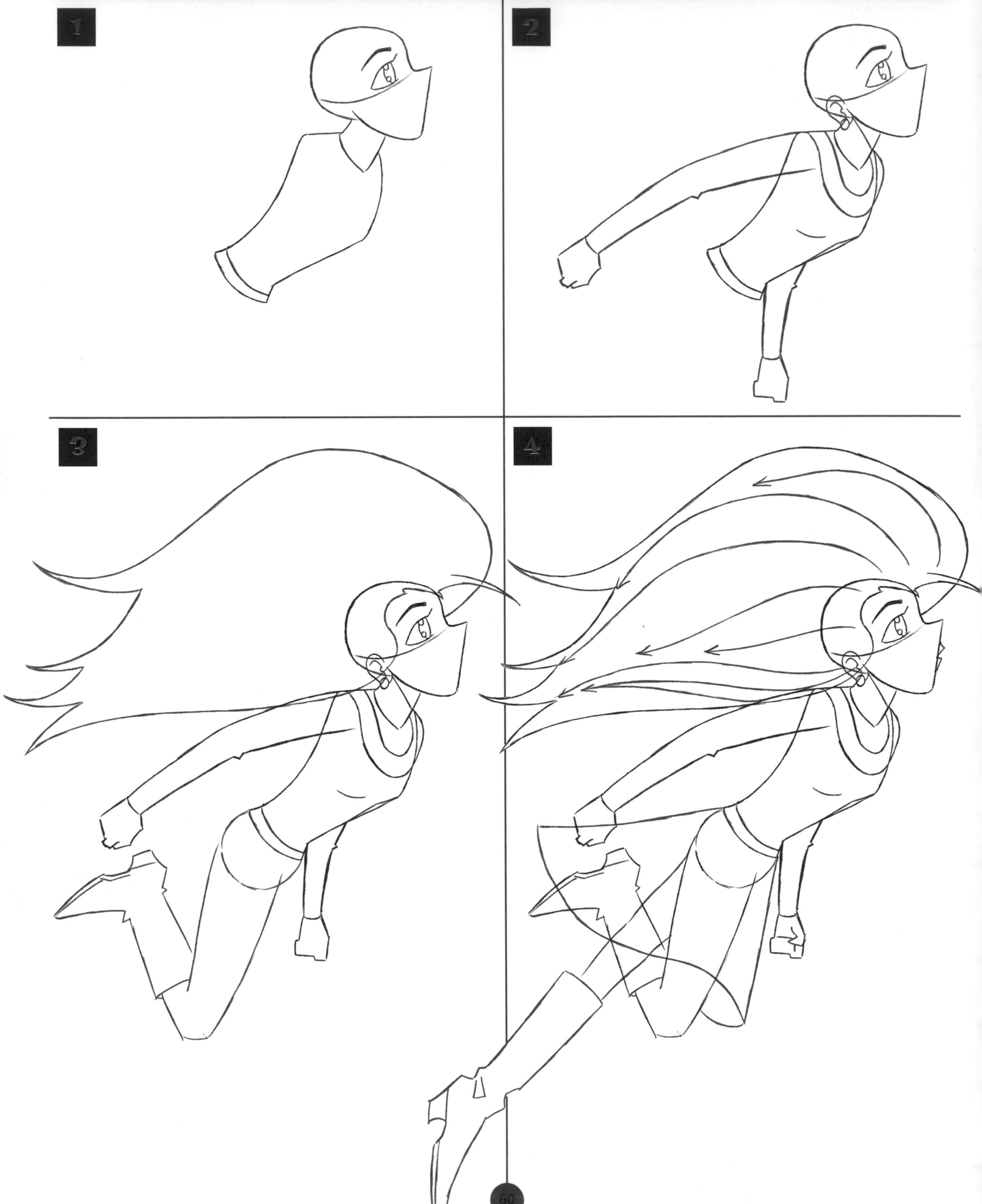
1
2
3
4

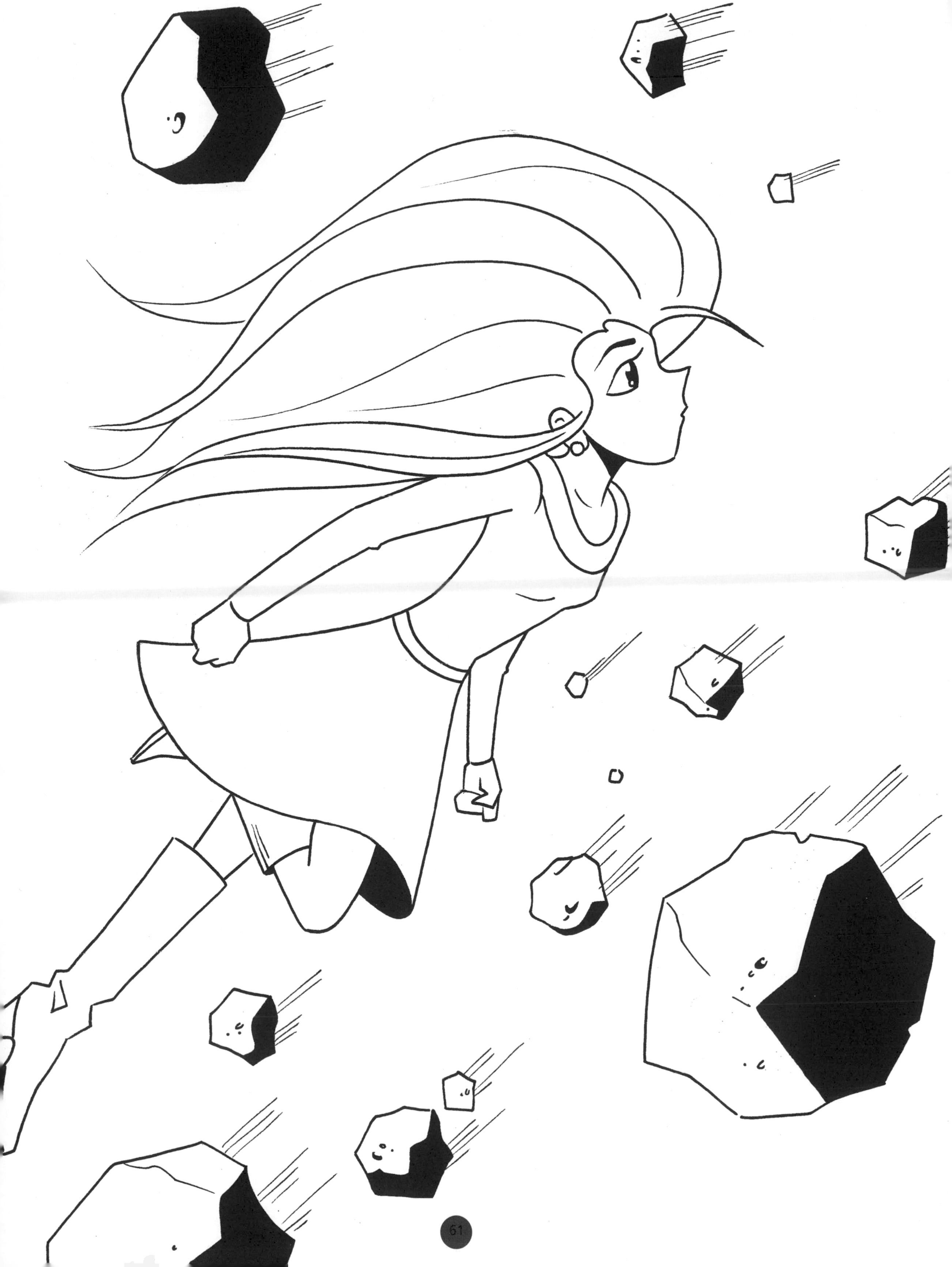

FLYING BOY

1

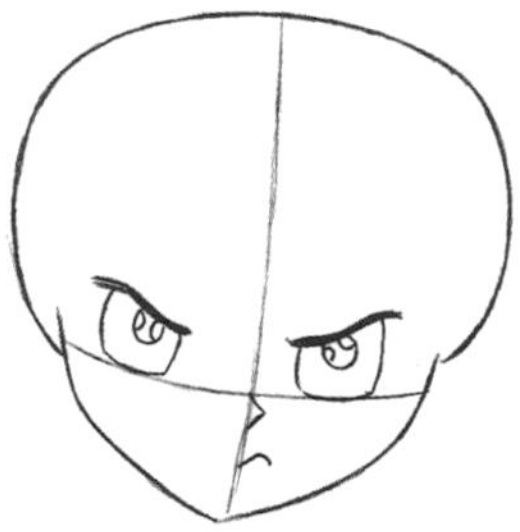

2

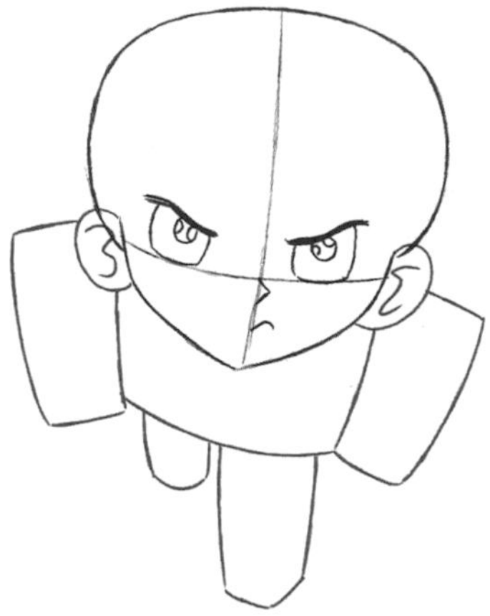

3

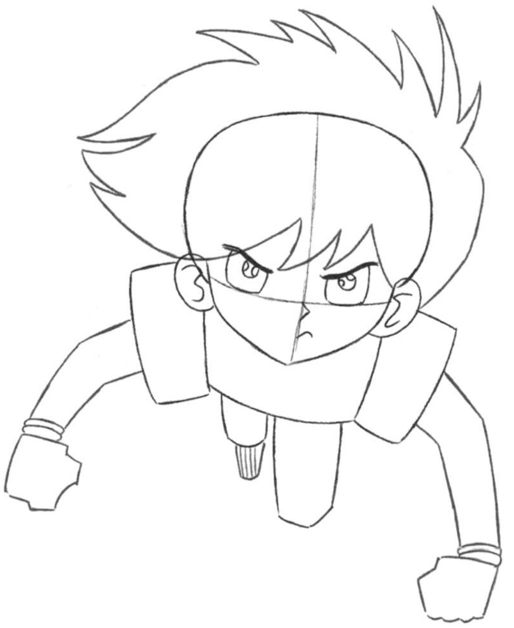

4

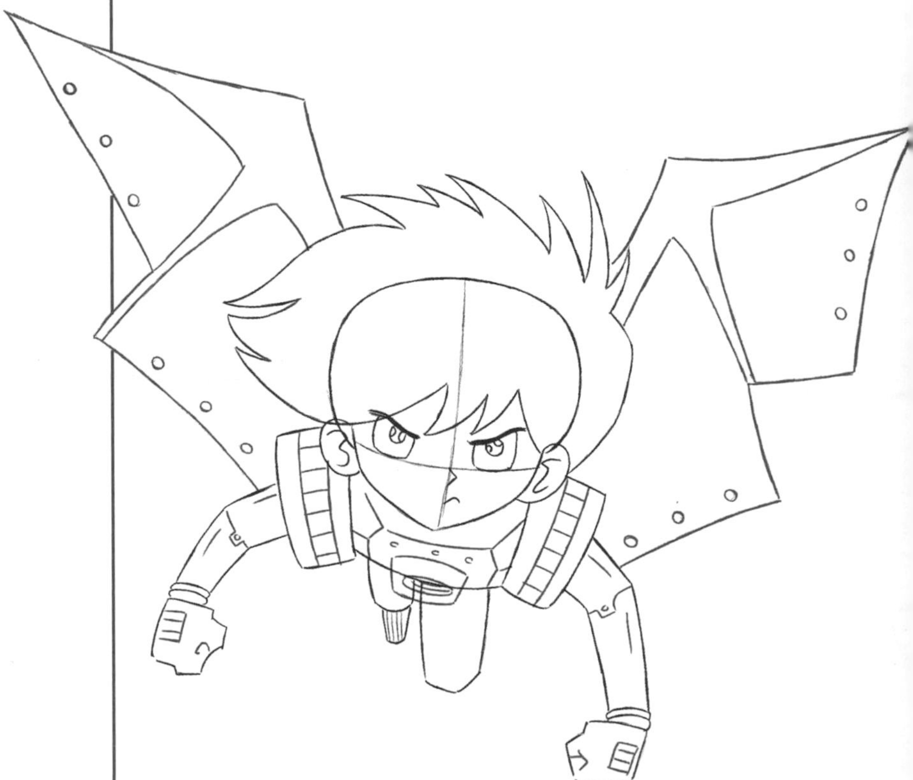

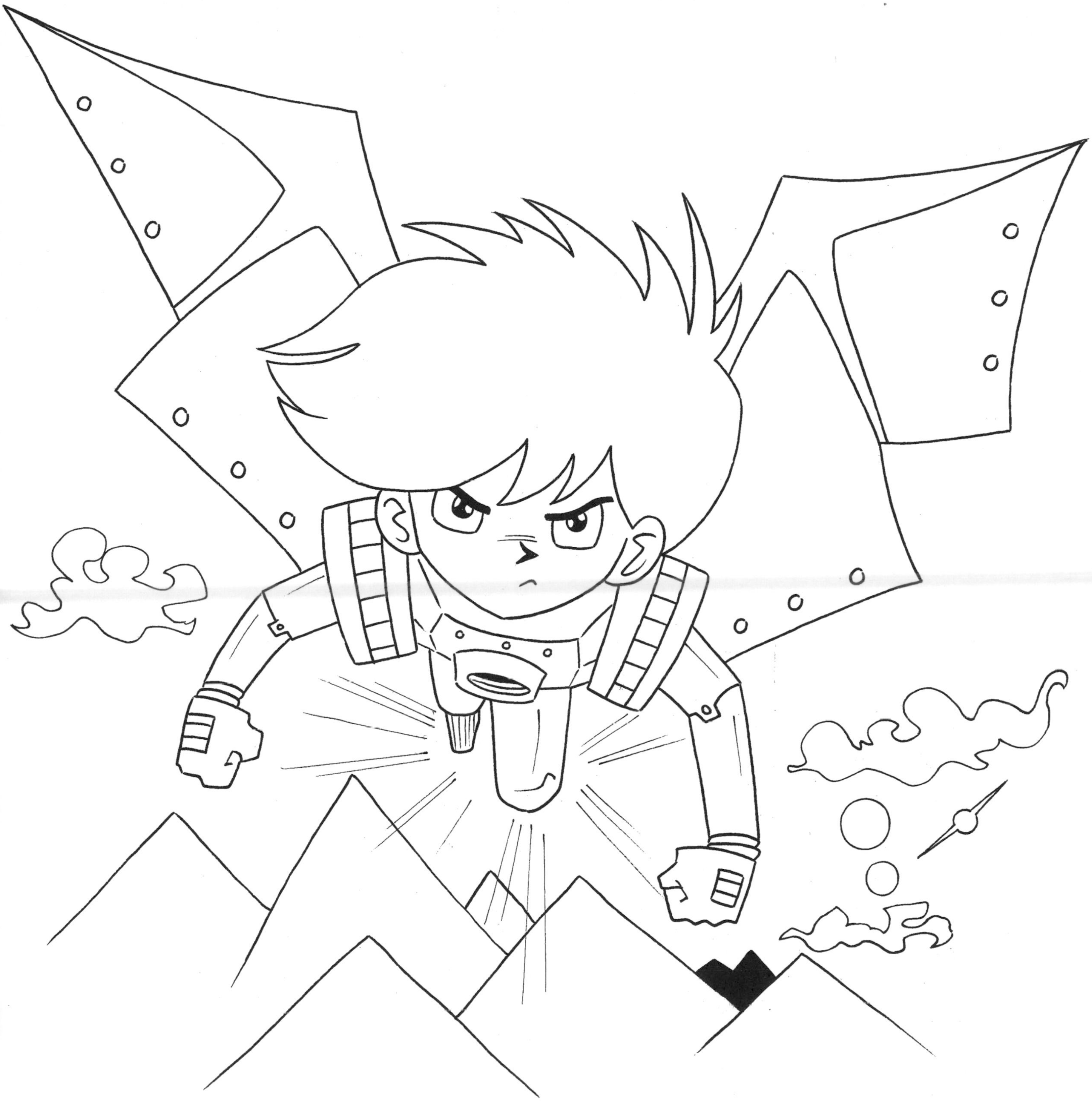

My thanks goes to all of the people who helped make this book possible:
Julie Mazur, Bob Ferro, Hector Campbell, and Bob Fillie.

I'd also like to thank Francesca Hart, for suggesting great names for the characters,
and Isabella Hart, for contributing her artistic judgment.

Senior Editor: Julie Mazur
Designer: Bob Fillie, Graphiti Design, Inc.
Production Manager: Hector Campbell
Text set in 13-pt Formata Regular

All drawings by Christopher Hart.

Cover art by Christopher Hart.
Text copyright © 2003 by Christopher Hart.
Illustrations copyright © 2003 by Christopher Hart.

First published in 2003 by
Watson-Guptill Publications,
Crown Publishing Group, a division of Random House Inc., New York
www.crownpublishing.com
www.watsonguptill.com

Library of Congress Cataloging-in-Publication Data
Hart, Christopher.
Draw manga! / by Christopher Hart.
p. cm. -- (Xtreme art)
Summary: Provides basic shapes and other techniques of cartooning,
followed by illustrated, step-by-step instructions for drawing cartoon
villains, superheroes, manga characters, and more.
ISBN 0-8230-0369-8
1. Cartooning--Technique--Juvenile literature. 2. Comic books,
strips, etc.--Japan--Technique--Juvenile literature. 3. Comic strip
characters--Juvenile literature. [1. Cartooning--Technique. 2.
Drawing--Technique. 3. Cartoons and comics.] I. Title.
NC1764.5.J3 H3692 2003
741.5--dc21   2003010662

Printed in China

First printing, 2003

7 8 / 11